Praise for *The Bigger Deal*

"Sunny Bindra is a big deal. Because he shares with relentless generosity and works to make the possibilities bigger for everyone he engages with."

Seth Godin, Author of *Linchpin*

"Sunny reveals some amazing insights and wisdom that can make every life the big deal it should be and the world a better place. He writes it as he has uniquely seen it and lived it. You won't put this book down."

Andrew Blacknell, Change and Communication Consultant (London) and co-author of *LEAD*

"*The Bigger Deal* encapsulates Sunny's own bigger deal: transforming the African work space by helping people shine an honest and often uncomfortable light on themselves. I have seen this lead to reinvention and recalibration in so many people and organizations. This book captures years and years of conversations and experiences. Recommended for professionals and entrepreneurs alike."

Carol Musyoka, Consultant, Educator and Columnist

"Sunny richly weaves common and uncommon sense to bring a new dimension to the old adage to 'aim high'— and beyond the self. Only then can we truly reach our potential and gain purpose and fulfilment in our life journeys. There is much to gain, so enjoy the book— and the ride."

Dr. Robin Kibuka, Chair, Standard Chartered Bank, Uganda, and Uganda Bureau of Statistics

"As long as I have known him, Sunny Bindra has persistently preached a life of purpose and significance. *The Bigger Deal* is an impassioned case for severing the shackles of mediocrity and pursuing a life that is extraordinary."

Jeenal Shah, Executive Director, AutoXpress Ltd.

"Sunny Bindra's book, *The Bigger Deal,* is a clarion call to action to all of us in our personal lives and in our spheres of influence. He challenges us to walk a path that will bring personal and professional fulfillment for ourselves, happiness to our families and friends, success to our organizations, prosperity to more in society and tolerance and peace in the world."

Lincoln Mali, Regional Head, Western Region, Standard Bank Group Africa

The **Bigger** Deal

with warm wishes

Sunny Bindra

WORK YOUR

WAY TO A LIFE

OF MEANING

Sunny Bindra

the BIG GER DEAL

Sunny Bindra
Nairobi, Kenya
www.sunwords.com

ISBN 978-9966-120-43-4 (paperback)
ISBN 978-9966-120-42-7 (ebook)

Produced by Page Two
www.pagetwostrategies.com
Editing by Jenny Govier
Cover design by Peter Cocking
Interior design by Taysia Louie

For all those who have a
deal bigger than themselves

Contents

Introduction
How Big Is Your Deal?

> **We're born, we live for a brief instant, and we die. It's been happening for a long time.**

STEVE JOBS

THE MEANING OF life is that it stops.

Eight very meaningful words from Franz Kafka. I read them years ago and experienced a pause.

Our time on this earth ends. In all cases, with no exceptions. There's a full stop. For some, this full stop intrudes early in the story. For others, the period comes at the end of a long, winding tome. But for all of us, life ends. We don't know when our full stop is coming. Really, we don't. We may expect to live seven decades or more, but that's just playing probabilities. You probably won't die tomorrow, but you certainly might. Whoever you are.

Is there life after the full stop? Perhaps there is. Some have faith to guide them beyond the full stop, others don't. The full stop in this life happens regardless of what we believe.

So then. This life is a short life. We don't have much time, and we don't know how much. So what are we going to do?

This simple question is what lies behind *The Bigger Deal*. Far from making us lose hope, Kafka's sentence should give us renewed vigour. What, indeed, are we going to do with this short, unpredictable life?

The answer is to make it a bigger deal. This brief, precious life should be a very big deal indeed, but so many of us settle for something far, far smaller. We settle for a deal in which we narrow our focus so much that we see nothing more than ourselves. A deal in which "me and mine" is the abiding credo. A deal in which we put on a mask of pretence to the world, faking concern and noble aims, when really all we want is self-gain. A deal in which we become conmen and spin doctors, tricking people into buying things that won't do much for them. A deal in which we value the flashy car for ourselves more than the process of creating value for others. A deal in which we fritter our time away in arguments and squabbles, petty scoring of points, nursing of much ill-will and many a perceived slight.

I watch many people do these things, incessantly and repetitively, and I wonder how much time they think they have to actually *live*. Life is short and precious; it should matter, and it should matter a great deal.

When we hear the word "deal," we naturally think "business." The world of business is indeed a key focus

Life is short and precious; it should matter, and it should matter a great deal.

of this book. Business should be a bigger deal. Most people on this planet work for businesses—their own, or in employment for businesses owned by others. Even if you have never worked for a business, however, if you think about it, business is a primal force in your life.

Business is the great engine of growth in the world; the primary creator of wealth; the key provider of employment for the people around you; the producer of the goods and services that make all our lives easier, more productive and more enjoyable. Business is actually a very big deal. When we take delight in a mouthful of cake in a favourite cafe or sit in the thrall of a riveting book, we are responding to pleasures created for us by someone's business. When we buy our first refrigerator or seek insurance for our belongings, we are trying to solve problems in our lives with the help of someone's business. When we reach for a smartphone to send an urgent message to a loved one or transfer money quickly, we are having our lives made easier by someone's business. And when we look for learning apps for our children or professional advice for ourselves, we are responding to the yearning for betterment that springs in every heart, and hoping that someone has devised a business that will deliver exactly that.

My continuing role in business is as a lifelong student, advisor, teacher and observer. I believe in the nobility of business. I believe that corporations can be a force for good in society. I believe many products are created that are of great utility for the ordinary person. I believe corporations can provide meaning and fulfilment for their employees, in a world largely devoid of meaning.

Much of the time, however, I am left aghast at the extent to which one of life's nobler pursuits is corrupted. Far from being the providers of value and opportunity to the world, too many of the world's business leaders seem to behave no better than hustlers on the street or crapshooters in the casino. They espouse a bigger deal for the cameras, but they are actually engaged in a very small deal indeed: all about the self rather than the collective; all about the personal bottom line rather than the impact on the planet.

The world is full of business scandal, every single day. Hype outstrips reality. The egos of a few take precedence over the interests of the many. Regulators are often found asleep at the wheel or in cahoots with big business. The media happily construct myths around larger-than-life business leaders. Professional advisors take the tainted coin and look the other way. The environment is exploited and ruined, and innocent people lose their lives so that a few rogues can make a few blood-soaked dollars.

It need not be that way. There is a bigger deal to play for. There is much more we can do with our businesses and our careers. This book is about that bigger deal: why it is worth pitching for, and what we have to do to realize it. It is about organizations that matter, that resonate, that last. It is about institutions and individuals who have a net positive impact on the planet: they make lives better.

The message that lives should be a bigger deal than most of them currently are is, I hope, one that will resonate far beyond boardrooms and management meetings. At its heart, *The Bigger Deal* is about the nature and meaning of work. In much of modern life we view work as a chore, a necessary evil, a means of earning income that allows us to truly "live" somewhere else. That view is only possible if we are lost in a small deal. When we are immersed in a bigger deal in life, we are completely in: absorbed fully in a cause that confers great meaning to our lives.

I have written *The Bigger Deal* in the hope that it will appeal to all those who want to make more of their lives and not just wallow in predictable mediocrity. That includes those who are thinking of starting their own businesses and those running established organizations, as well as those working for them. But the book is really a book about meaning: beyond personal profits; beyond the exchange of "labour" for "compensation"; beyond the mundanity of an existence that just goes through the motions and is then extinguished.

How big is *your* deal? Are you here to play big? Can you think beyond personal, short-term gain? Are you ready to use your time on earth to create wider

> When we are immersed in a bigger deal in life, we are completely in: absorbed fully in a cause **that confers great meaning to our lives.**

benefits? Will you leave something of lasting value behind when you're gone? I hope this book will prompt you to think about how big your deal is—and how to make it bigger.

The Bigger Deal is for those who want to use this short life to work, really work, on something that emerges from deeply held, passionate beliefs.

1

The
Small Deal

Stop chasing the money, and start chasing the passion.

TONY HSIEH

WHERE WE SEE
WHAT A **SMALL DEAL**
LOOKS LIKE.

YOU'RE THINKING OF starting a business, because you never want to work for anyone else. You recognize that you don't have any original ideas, but why should that stop you? Your aim is to be rich and envied, and there are many ways to do that. You start off by launching a company that mimics most of the established players in the industry, with very similar products. The only difference is that your products are cheaper, because you have found a way to cut corners on the raw materials without the customer noticing. Your products won't last as long as your competitors' ones do, but you know there's a big chunk of customers who will go for the lower price.

And so you're off, and sales start to grow. You need more employees, but you really don't want to pay over the odds. So you look for recently qualified graduates and diploma holders who won't ask for too much money. Given what you pay, you don't really expect to hold on to your staff—but that's OK; there are always plenty more where they came from. All you want is their labour, after all—the business is yours.

You also managed to find a supplier who gave you a very good deal on second-hand machinery—why pay more than you need to when it's less profit in your pocket if you do? And let these branded companies have their swanky offices—your premises are in a seedy part of town. Your three dozen staff have to share a single washroom, and only the front of the building is painted—who looks at the back, anyway? Your own office is nicely kitted out, though, with carpets, a big-screen TV, and a private executive toilet.

Your sales are good, powered by low prices. The fact that you save so much on inputs gives you an even higher profit margin than competitors who charge much more. Customers can't really tell the difference in quality between the rival products, at least not initially. You don't really entertain any complaints, though—people who pay that little should not expect superior service.

And so you become cash-rich fairly soon. You buy a BMW immediately, and all your friends and family members are openly envious. It feels good. You start looking around for other opportunities—after all, you don't really have any connection to this particular industry. It was just an opportunity. The alert entrepreneur should always be looking around for other breaks, no? An insurance-broker friend of yours is looking for investors, and he has a captive market—he sells to government agencies where he has deep contacts. You're thinking of delaying your machinery upgrade to send some money his way. Every savvy operator knows diversification is the essence of business.

. . .

YOU ARE A senior executive in a large conglomerate. You have all the right credentials: an accounting degree, and an MBA from a top school. Not to mention the experience: this is your sixth position in the same industry. You've been very clever about it—you've always moved for a higher remuneration package by being a canny negotiator and ensuring you have board members rooting for you.

Your trump card is that you deliver seemingly real results: the quarterly numbers that every CEO and board is judged on. You've been in the game long enough to know exactly how that's done. Amplify the challenges you face and the mess your predecessor created; pitch low on targets, and then surprise everyone; book revenues before their time, and delay accounting for costs; peg your bonuses to the profit targets; and finally, leave the company before the numbers catch up with you. You never expect to stay longer than two or three years, in any case. You're not wedded to these shareholders; why sweat your own life out for them?

You despise the group CEO, your boss. They're all the same—in it for themselves, while pretending to be "inclusive" or building "ownership" or "shared rewards." If only the ordinary employees knew how big the CEO's bonus was! You make it your business to find that out in every new job you take. A few expensive drinks in your club for one of the accountants is usually enough to extract that useful little piece of information. Knowing what the boss gouges out of the enterprise is vital in negotiating your own annual bonus.

As for the customers... oh dear, what a bunch of whiners. They seem to think they have the right to enslave you, just because they paid a few measly dollars for one of your products. Honestly, the sense of entitlement they have... you don't have any time for them, but in this social-media and viral-video era one has to be careful. You pay a great deal for a digital agency to run your many social channels and tweet and post platitudes all day long on the company's behalf. Inspirational quotations seem to work especially well. You yourself say all the right things in your speeches: "customer-centricity," "shared value," "employees first," and other buzzwords. And you always remember to thank your customers profusely every time your organization wins an award, which is very often (you pay handsomely to sponsor awards ceremonies).

Life is good. You have a top-of-the-range SUV, and the company pays for your kids to go to the best schools. Golf twice a week is easily done. But you just saw a remuneration survey in the newspaper that suggests you aren't in the very top tier of salaries in the market. That's quite unsettling. Maybe it's time to brush up the resumé and start dropping hints in the members' bar...

. . .

YOU WERE POOR as a child, and you never want to go back there again. You often had to subsist on a single meal per day and were sometimes sent home from school because your parents had been unable to come up with the school fees. As a teenager, you had to look on in envy as your friends went to the movies.

Nonetheless, you worked hard at your studies and managed to get the right qualifications. Decades later, you are in a secure job earning in the upper percentiles of the income range for your line of work. Your own children are well looked after. You should feel secure and comfortable. But do you?

Actually, you still find yourself obsessing over money. You are constantly mulling over your investment statements to work out whether you'll have enough to retire on once your children's university education is paid for. You wonder what it will be like to live off a fixed sum again and have to abstain from the little luxuries you've become used to. You take on additional work for the overtime, do a little moonlighting here and there, and fight bitterly for your annual bonus to be higher.

You've never really been able to stop thinking about money. You chastise your children all the time for not appreciating how hard you work to pay for their things. You always question the price you have to pay, and always try to negotiate it downwards. You look for the cheapest hotel deals when going on holiday and wait for the annual sales before buying your clothes.

You feel great joy when you believe you've cleverly found a bargain and acute anxiety when you think you paid too much. You tip people precisely, but never generously. You never give to charity if you can't claim the donation as an expense. You've never bought a new car, because you always let some other mug pay the first two years' depreciation.

You fret a lot and never seem to enjoy yourself with your family and friends. You calculate carefully an appropriate amount to spend on everything, even on gifts for your spouse. Those close to you often tell you to let go once in a while—but that doesn't make sense to you. You must get value from everything. You tell yourself it's because you've had to work hard for your money all your life—no one gave it you on a plate, unlike some people. But you do sometimes wonder why you've really never enjoyed your life...

" You do sometimes wonder why you've **really never enjoyed your life . . .** "

"

Small deals have nothing to do with the size of the balance sheet. **They are all about the size of the spirit within.**

"

Trapped in a Small Deal

In case it wasn't obvious, all the people described above are trapped in a small deal. None of them think so—they are, after all, relatively successful and affluent folk. But small deals have nothing to do with the size of the balance sheet. They are all about the size of the spirit within.

That's the thing with the small deal: on the surface, it doesn't always look like one. Some of the world's biggest corporations and richest people are small dealers. Many people engaged in small deals give off the aura of success: they flaunt the trappings and trinkets of having made it; they walk confidently and talk big. Where they are small, however, is deep inside.

People who are ensnared in a small deal in life are here to take, not to give. They aim to maximize their own pleasures and accomplishments at the expense of everyone else. They don't understand "win-win." They can only win by beating others—by tricking, exploiting or outwitting them. For them, life is a game of extraction. You pluck what you can from this planet and its inhabitants while you're alive. And then you die. What could be smaller than that?

There are many ways to be caught in the small deal. Small deals are happening all over the place, as people trade generosity for selfishness and achievements for accoutrements. Small dealers are all around you—in boardrooms and boudoirs; shouting on street corners as well as in the highest offices.

So what does a small deal look like? Let's consider some common characteristics.

It's all about you: Deals are small when they are structured to make you the primary beneficiary. Other players in the deal are accessories, there to be used or hoodwinked. Your key aim is to do something for yourself—your wealth, your status, your power. "Me and mine" is your mantra. Personal gain is the desired outcome.

It has hollow outcomes: The hallmark of the small deal is the vapidity of the desired outcome. Small dealers are obsessed with small results: the bulging bank account; the trophy car; the golf-club membership. They never think of higher-level results and don't understand people who do. Creating wider wellbeing or uplift for others is an alien concept to the small dealer.

It won't last: Small deals can look good, but only for a short period. Businesses run by small dealers are eventually found out. Employees never stick around, and customers soon become tired of complaining. A deal that does not create value for all is weak and vulnerable, and is soon abandoned by those tricked into participating. A deal that is aimed at exploiting a scarce resource,

Creating wider wellbeing or uplift for others is an alien concept to the small dealer.

such as the environment or talented employees, crumbles once the resource is exhausted.

It's stressful: People trapped in small deals are also trapped in anxiety and tension. Deep down, they know their castles are built on sand, and so they always fear losing them. No matter how much money they have, money worries dog them all their lives. The hallmarks of the small dealer are ever-shifting eyes, mistrust, irritability and the insomnia that living in perpetual tension always brings.

IN ALL THESE respects, the card-sharp hustling on the street is little different from the big-bank CEO playing with toxic debt instruments on the thirtieth floor above. The conman selling cure-all medicines to gullible or desperate people on the internet is little different from the owner of the trucking company deliberately scrimping on maintenance costs and making his drivers work ungodly hours. They may dress differently and command different attention in society, but they're small dealers, all.

We all have some drops of the small dealer in us. The trick is to recognize the many traps that make us think and play small. Bigness begins right there.

2

Start with
Purpose

The mystery of human existence lies not in just staying alive, but in finding something to live for.

FYODOR DOSTOYEVSKY

WHERE WE LEARN
TO HAIL THE
MONOMANIACS.

WHAT'S THE POINT of your life? Do you know? What are you here to do—what's your mission on earth?

Most of us haven't got the faintest clue. Most of us just exist, until we don't. We barely pause to think there might be a point to this existence, one that's right here, not contingent on the promise of heaven elsewhere.

Most of us move from one event in our lives to the next, barely pausing to reflect or take stock. We meet people, begin relationships, gain qualifications, get jobs, start businesses, advance a little, face reversals, change direction, keep going... until there's nothing more to do. Most of us are very busy indeed: some of us busy in the process of trying to survive; others busy in the process of trying to thrive. Whether we're surviving or thriving, though, we don't get the point of anything. It's a race to the graveyard, in which we win nothing at the end.

When that end comes, people gather to send you off. One minute, you are fully alive on earth, working, contributing, connecting; the next, due to some often surprising (or mostly predictable) turn of events, you are gone. You are no more, with people gathered around your lifeless form to record the passing.

Other people's funerals are a good place for deeper thought. Observing endings is a suitable time to dwell on the meaning of your own life. Many people experience a moment of realization during a funeral; most, however, walk away brushing it off. They get back to their lives, get on with their work, make themselves busy—anything to not have to think about the thing, that unsettling, scary thing. And the thing is this: we are all, all of us, insignificant. It doesn't matter whose eulogy is being delivered: whether it's a loyal employee or a respected CEO; a plumber or an epoch-creating president. It's all the same. In the end, all earthly achievements fade away. Life goes on. People move on. Memories fade. None of us wants to accept this, yet all of us must.

No individual human seems to matter. You are one in seven point five billion, living on a piece of rock floating in the immenseness of a space we can neither measure nor comprehend. You are a speck, alive briefly on another speck. Sure, you will matter briefly to a few people, but in the end, you too will be washed away by the waves of time.

Very few of us want to think about this. Most of us want to lose ourselves in a TV show, hide behind a book, gratify ourselves momentarily by indulging the senses of the body. Do something, anything, except give some thought to how this story, like all such stories, ends. Until the next funeral. And the next. Until, inevitably, our own.

Talking about death, thinking about it, discussing it, is one of those strange taboos in society. Many of you may in fact be recoiling from reading these paragraphs. But you can't have taboos about things that are unavoidable facts. Life, as comedian John Cleese is said to have put it, is a sexually transmitted terminal disease. We should laugh as we accept the inevitability of the end.

The point, though, is the significance of your insignificance. One outcome of deep contemplation is to fall into deep lethargy. If it all just ends and nothing matters, then what's the point? Many an existential crisis is triggered by embracing mortality. Albert Camus famously pointed out that human life is just the same as pushing a rock up a hill, as Sisyphus was condemned to do, only to watch it roll down, and then repeating the process over and over again. It is absurd.

Everyone is pushing the rock, from the mother cooking yet another meal for her child, to the chief executive poring over yet another spreadsheet to present to his investors, to the columnist churning out yet another piece for yet another edition. All the rocks will come rolling back.

So far, so gloomy.

As I wrote above, we are, all of us, just "a speck on a speck." I have never forgotten those words. They were uttered by a teacher in my presence many years ago. But here's the thing: he wasn't referring to some bacterium sitting on a rock in the ocean, or a particle of space dust in some far-off galaxy.

He was referring to *me*.

The teacher had asked me to tell him about myself. I recounted a quick resumé of my life to date, including all the details I thought impressive: my education, upbringing, occupation, work achievements. To which the good teacher replied, "Just as I thought: you are a speck on a speck."

After I had gathered myself, he went on to explain: "The planet Earth is but a mere speck in the huge universe. You are but a mere speck of life on this Earth. So that is what you are: a speck on a speck. Don't take yourself at all seriously."

The idea that there is only one life in this universe, and that we—in common with the birds, the trees, the stars—are but one speck of this life has long been known by the greater and wiser men and women who have walked amongst us. To have any meaning, we

> You are **a speck on a speck.**

" Once you have understood that you will probably amount to nothing, you're **ready to amount to something.** "

must be part of a bigger whole. To have any importance, we must be an element in a bigger idea. In themselves, our lives are irrelevant events in the maelstrom of existence. Scary, isn't it?

In this hyper-competitive world, we are all brought up and trained and groomed to think of ourselves as something, not nothing. The idea that we are just floating dust, that we amount to nothing, that we are, at the end of the day, irrelevant—that's not comfortable. But we have to become uncomfortable before enlightenment can possibly dawn.

I run a leadership course. On day one every year, the assembled renowned chief executives, accomplished managers and high-flying entrepreneurs are introduced to one another and then shown a slide with the assertion: You are a speck on a speck.

They find this difficult. Many resist, or try to find an escape clause that allows them to be more than a speck. There isn't one. I have mentored leaders who have introduced breakthrough products that have changed entire industries, who have had a positive impact on the lives of millions. It doesn't matter who they are. They're still specks. So am I. So, certainly, are you.

At the end of the day, I am just one of many billions of people on this planet. This planet is itself one of untold billions in the universe. So I am indeed utterly insignificant in the grand scheme of things. No matter how much I achieve, I am expendable and forgettable.

Stay with me; there's better news coming.

The mere acceptance of our insignificance opens up the door to significance. Once you have understood that you will probably amount to nothing, you're ready to amount to something. Here's the thing: you can make yourself matter. You can remain a speck on a speck but still have a point to your existence and an impact in your life. The exhortation that you are nothing is not intended to deflate or discourage you; it is meant to fire you up to make something meaningful out of your life on this planet. The realization that you don't matter is what will release you to make yourself matter.

Why do I insist that leaders coming to my course first admit their insignificance? Because an inflated sense of self is the root of many problems. It makes people smug and complacent. Once you feel happy with your accomplishments to date, you are going to feel already capable, already wise, already knowing it all. You will arrive with your cup of learning already full, and nothing else will go in. The idea that there is a self—a distinctive, individual self—is deemed by many thinkers to itself be a delusion. We confuse the ego—a construct of the mind—with the self.

Accepting that you are a speck on a speck takes you to the next question: so now what? A little thought may then reveal an important insight: sure, none of us is more than a speck. But the specks, viewed collectively, do matter. No one mortal has been indispensable in the course of history, yet the history of mankind is a wondrous thing. It is full of enormous intellectual, artistic and economic achievements. That stream of significance is caused by billions of elements insignificant in themselves. The ocean, as a totality, is a thing of wonder. An individual wave, plant or creature in that ocean is not.

This is how we must view our lives: I can't ever amount to much, but *we* certainly can.

Hail the Monomaniacs

Let's climb down from the mountaintop of abstract thinking and come down into the valley where real people live. What do you make of a man who created employment—and, therefore, livelihoods—for two million others? What do you think of another man who took his country from a third-world swamp to a first-world economic powerhouse in just one generation? What reflections do you have on a woman who resisted the medieval patriarchy into which she was born and led her nation on an entirely unexpected cause: that of planting trees and protecting the environment?

Those people were, respectively, Sam Walton, who created Walmart, the world's biggest retailer; Lee Kuan Yew, founding prime minister of Singapore;

and Wangari Maathai, founder of Kenya's Green Belt Movement.

You don't have to engage in blind adulation to accept that these lives mattered. Sam Walton's Walmart is often in the news for all the wrong reasons—usually concerning disputes regarding its pay practices. Lee Kuan Yew was notably authoritarian and elitist in his approach to his country's development. Wangari Maathai may have got Kenyans to plant millions of trees, but she did not create an enduring respect for the environment in her country.

Does any of that matter, though? The three were human beings, fallible and flawed, just like the rest of us. The interesting thing is not to point out their many shortcomings, but rather to marvel at the drive that took them to mind-boggling achievement. And at the centre of that achievement is a deep sense of purpose.

Sam Walton grew up in the dust bowl of Depression-ridden America. For a large part of his life he was just another shopkeeper running a corner store. There was little sign in the early days that he would become one of the world's richest men, founder of America's biggest private employer. But he was propelled by a central purpose in his life: to change the face of American retailing. His big idea was about price and convenience—the lowest prices, the most locations. This idea consumed him. It became his reason for living. Walmart's stated purpose—"To save people money so they can live better"—captures the calling that Sam instilled. And with one-third of Americans currently visiting Walmart every week, that purpose has seemed to resonate.

Lee Kuan Yew was, by many accounts, a haughty and intolerant man. But he had a singular achievement, one that few will ever match. During his tenure as founder-leader of Singapore, that country was taken from being a few scattered fishing islands on the tip of the Malay Peninsula to one of the world's richest and most well-organized countries. From third world to first in a single generation. He did this by single-mindedly imposing order and discipline on his society, by stamping out corruption and by opening up his tiny nation to the world. A driven man, he brooked no dissent and attracted many detractors. But there is no doubting the achievement. A look at Singapore's neighbours shows the difference that a single committed leader can make, even when the odds are stacked against him.

Wangari Maathai grew up in a tiny Kenyan village in the 1940s, her father a poor tenant farmer at a time when few girls were educated. Through sheer force of will, she got herself schooled, excelling in her studies and winning scholarships to the United States. In 1971 she became one of the first women in Africa to obtain a doctorate, and a few years later she founded the Green Belt Movement with two aims: to empower her nation's women and to protect its environment. The movement is credited with the planting of more than 30 million trees in Kenya and providing roughly 30,000 women with new skills and opportunities. She did this against huge opposition from the country's draconian ruling party of the time, often getting beaten up and bloodied in the process. Maathai was given the 2004 Nobel Peace Prize for "her contribution to sustainable development, democracy and peace."

These people are monomaniacs. They had an over-whelming obsession with just one thing: cheaper shopping; economic development; planting trees. They devoted their entire lives to their one thing. They were knocked down, and they stood up again. They kept going and going, until the thing that was their thing was a done thing.

With Purpose Behind You

The present world is full of examples of purpose-driven leaders who create success around them.

Apple has been the world's most valuable company for years now. Its original purpose—"Making tools for the mind that advance humankind"—came from its iconic founder, Steve Jobs. A manic perfectionist, he could tolerate no product that lacked "taste" and that could not be used with ease by anyone. That intense focus on the user experience is what drives Apple.

Steve Jobs's great achievement was not profits and market capitalization; it was to make his products matter in the lives of his customers.

IKEA serves nearly 800 million visitors in its stores and clocks nearly a billion visits to its website every year. The innovative Swedish furniture retailer, founded by Ingvar Kamprad in 1943 at the age of seventeen, truly changed how furniture was made and sold. Again, there is purpose at work here: Kamprad was hell-bent from the outset on making his products not just cheap, but really cheap. This forced him to break industry norms and seek non-traditional manufacturers, design huge hangar-sized display and collection stores, and pioneer the flat-pack self-assembly model that cut out a whole swathe of costs from the final price. Kamprad was famous for saying one thing over and over: that IKEA's idea was "to create a better everyday life for the many people." This purpose is real, not just vapid wishful thinking. IKEA is one of the few companies whose products actually go down in price every year on average. In a testament he wrote, Kamprad stated IKEA had "decided once and for all to side with the many." In other words, it would not waver from the mission of providing very affordable furniture to the great majority—but would do it with some distinction and panache.

WhatsApp did not exist before 2009, but it has now become the world's most popular messaging service having crossed the landmark figure of one billion active users in 2017. As you will have picked up by now, there is purpose at play here, too. Its astonishing growth is not caused by clever marketing; the product went viral because it fulfilled a real need in the world. Communication is a universal good: every one of us needs to keep in touch with other people, for work or play. What's interesting about WhatsApp is the reason its uptake was so phenomenal. That reason is in the product, which is cheap, almost free; is simple to sign up to and use; and allows the user to create groups and share a wide variety of media. Instant mass communication, in other words. WhatsApp message volume now far exceeds the total SMS messages handled by all telcos in the world.

It's amazing what you can achieve when you have a purpose behind you, rather than just a need to make money. The former gives you guidance, direction and resolve; the latter makes you change course repeatedly and make compromises at every stage.

Lack of purpose leads inexorably to small deals. It causes us to meander everywhere, seeking meaning in mimicry and needing validation from all and sundry. People with purpose are different. They stay the course. They resist temptation. They refuse to compromise. They do not accept a different path, no matter how much easier it is to follow. They are beaten down and beaten back by all those invested in the status quo. But

It's amazing what you can achieve when you have a purpose behind you.

> **Life is a meandering** and meaningless junket when it lacks purpose.

they bounce back up again and again, and they keep going. Their life has meaning only in relation to their purpose in living it.

I do not mean to suggest that the organizations highlighted here exemplify everlasting success and achievement. Walmart's best days may already be behind it (it is reeling from the onslaught of another purpose-driven behemoth, Amazon); Apple competes in brutally competitive markets, and competitors are fast closing the gap in key products; and WhatsApp's original ethos has changed after being acquired by Facebook. Missteps and reversals will undoubtedly occur. Business is like that. The deeper point is that a collective sense of purpose can lead to astonishing results within a lifetime, and that individuals who can instill and channel that purpose are very valuable indeed.

What's the Point of Your Life?

So I ask again: what's the point of your life? Do you know? What are you here to do?

It's not for everyone, this sense of driving purpose. Most people are not going ever to really have one. The best they can hope for is to be enrolled in someone else's mission on earth, rather than their own. And that's fine, too. Not everyone can be a visionary or a coordinator or a coach. Some of us have to be enjoined in a purpose.

But enjoined we must be. Life is a meandering and meaningless junket when it lacks purpose. We move from one thing to another, losing interest, being inattentive, living to low standards. Without purpose, we have no belief system, no propeller. We just... are.

I may have described some daunting, iconic figures in this chapter. My intention is not to exhort you to be like them. I chose them because they show what is possible: that people of unsuitable backgrounds in inopportune times can rise up and make a real ding in the universe (to use Steve Jobs's unforgettable phrase).

Most of us will not found game-changing institutions or alter the course of history. But most of us do need to address the question, "What's the point of my life? Do I know?"

Sometimes, the answer to that question is found by being a meaningful cog in a bigger machine. The next chapter shows how.

3

Earn a Life,
Not Just a Living

"

They pretend to pay us an honest wage and we pretend to do an honest day's work.

HUNGARIAN JOKE

"

WHERE WE DISCOVER
THAT **EMPLOYMENT** CAN
BE A VERY BIG DEAL.

YOU HAVE BEEN doing the same job for five years, without any promotion or meaningful increase in pay. You know why that is. The world is inherently unfair. It favours some people, and leaves others on the dustheap. Your parents were not rich. They were not able to give you a university education or leave you any money. And so you sit in a dead-end job with no prospects. There's no point in working hard—it's never rewarded. The game is rigged. Your boss favours his own appointees whatever you do.

So you sit in the same seat year after year. You do just enough work to avoid getting sacked. Why should you do any more than that? Don't give these exploiters any more of yourself than they're entitled to. Earn your pay, and that's it.

You feel very bitter, though, about how your life is working out. You complain a lot. You watch younger people come in with their fancy qualifications and see how quickly they get promoted. Some of them become your superiors, even though they're just smug little know-it-alls. If you'd had their advantages in life...

You can't stand people who tell you to be positive. What the hell do they know about what it's like to be in your life? Either they've got themselves a very nice deal and now they're being condescending to everyone else, or they're just vapid feel-good types with no sense of reality in them. If people want to know what life is really like, they should talk to you. Few people do, though. To hell with them.

The Phenomenal Flight Attendant

I have encountered many flight attendants in my time, mostly mediocre, some good. Ioana belongs in the "outstanding" category. Long flights are often a good chance to catch up with one's reading. On a recent flight, however, I abandoned my valuable hoard of reading material simply to watch Ioana in action.

This lady was phenomenally engaged with her work. Being a flight attendant, please note, is way less glamorous a job than most people think it is. You are indeed technically trained to be a safety officer and a leader in a crisis, but much of the time you are forced to be a glorified maid, usher and waiter combined: heating and serving food; cleaning up after people; herding them; listening to incessant requests and complaints. And that experience is repeated day after day. It is very difficult to keep smiling through it all.

Not so with Ioana. She was a dynamo radiating positive energy in everything she did. She fetched and carried; she served and cleared up; she played with children; she responded to every query. Most importantly, she seemed to be exactly the same with every type of customer: every race, every background, every social class.

The Blessed of the Earth

Most employees are more like the first person described in this chapter, not like Ioana. What makes her special? What makes her so able to do this job with such distinction, when most of her peers in other airlines are so poor at it?

The first answer to this question is a personal deal. People like Ioana are indeed special. They set high individual standards for themselves, and they do things well for their own pleasure and satisfaction, not because they are made to by someone else.

I am always telling chief executives and recruiters that people like these are like gold dust: look out for them and hire them without too many questions when you encounter them. The person with a positive out-look and inner drive and high standards can only do good for your organization, especially when placed in front of customers.

The second answer is about organizational culture. People like Ioana thrive when they are in the right environment. Ioana works for an airline that features regularly in the world's top ten for passenger-service excellence. Ioana was undoubtedly outstanding—but she was surrounded by very able colleagues, mostly dis-playing similar energy and engagement. That can only be because she is part of a culture and system, driven by leadership, that creates excellence.

Great customer experience happens when great individuals and great organizational cultures come together. The quality of the person certainly matters, but so do the standards and norms set by the orga-nization. A remarkable organization aims to find and develop many, many Ioanas, not just one. It spots them, encourages them, rewards them and uses them to set the tone.

Surveys repeatedly indicate that out of every ten employees, only one or two will be actively enjoying their work or willing to do anything extra for their employer or customer. Highly engaged employees are very rare across the globe. Meeting such employees is invariably heartwarming. They are good for cus-tomers, good for their fellow employees, and good for

" People who enjoy
their work are truly the
blessed of the earth.
"

shareholders. They usually go far and create great net positive value in the world.

People who enjoy their work are truly the blessed of the earth. They get up every day buzzing with energy and feel they are in the right place doing the right thing. How many of us can claim to be like that?

This places a great responsibility on us: to find the work we will love doing, and to simultaneously love the idea of work. Most people are imprisoned by their own bad attitudes, festering in dead-end jobs with bad organizations.

There is a better way to live and work. Unfortunately, our idea of work is so stilted and jaded that we kill off all enthusiasm in most of our people.

The Small Deal in Employment

Here's the deal. We offer you employment in our organization. You will provide your labour, and we'll pay you in return. But please note some basic points very carefully.

The organization belongs to us, not you. It exists to fulfil our purpose and push our agenda, not yours. You are a hired hand, a cog in our machine. You follow instructions. You are not asked to think, just to do as you're told. We will provide all the manuals and directions that you need. If you follow them diligently, we will keep paying you, at slightly higher rates every year.

You will probably hate your work with us. We know that. It will be repetitive and banal, because we keep the interesting stuff for ourselves. We don't really expect you to be terribly lively while working, as long as you do it. Just clock in and clock out.

You will come to life elsewhere, not here. You will live for the weekends, when you are able to be alive: with your family, with the boys at the bar, watching the big game or singing with great zeal at church.

You will always say "Thank God it's Friday" and "I hate Mondays." Five-sevenths of your life will be forced labour. That is why you are called a human "resource." And that is why what we pay you will be called "compensation"—it is recompense for taking a big chunk out of your life. Because there is no meaning to what you do, we recognize that money will be the only reason you work for us. A little more money offered elsewhere is all it will take for you to leave us. That's fine too—there are plenty more where you came from.

You will be part of a large crowd. Out of this crowd, we will handpick a very small number for elevation. The criteria for elevation will include your capacity for sycophancy, your willingness to play the game by our rules and your ability to manipulate others. If you play your cards right, you may be chosen to join the elite group known as "senior management." Your key responsibility now will be to keep the game going on our behalf and quell any rebellions. For this you will be paid more, something we will call "reward and remuneration."

Let's stop there. Did I just describe your job or your organization? Even if you deny it, the chances are good that I did: as indicated earlier, global surveys repeatedly reveal that only a small minority of workers are truly engaged in their work with any enthusiasm. And this isn't just about low-level labourers; the malaise goes all the way to the top in many organizations. Other surveys show that between a third and a half of employees in organizations are ready to leave at any given time if anything better comes up.

Why do we do this? Why is this the only employment contract we are able to offer, even if we pretend otherwise? Because our view of employment is stuck in the era when we needed worker-drones to come to the fields and mills and factories and do as they were told by the clever people. Most people were indeed just resources then.

Look around you. How many people are truly at work? How many feel engaged and alive, connected with their work, ready to give their best, imbued with a sense of meaning and purpose? Not many.

Most employment is mostly awful. It requires you to park your humanity at the door and walk in as a human "resource," and exchange unwilling labour in return for monetary compensation. Why is it like this? Because our attitudes toward management and work are rooted in a long-dead past: a past in which there were a few rich, educated, clever people and huge armies of poor,

" Most employment is mostly awful. It requires you to park your humanity at the door **and walk in as a human 'resource.'** "

uneducated, ignorant people. The former naturally organized the latter as "resources," in the same way they organized equipment and machinery.

That era, thankfully, is fading away. Human beings are way more educated, way more knowledgeable, way more exposed and way more connected than they were in that time of mass ignorance. In most organizations today, we can't expect employees to be cheap, plentiful, undemanding and expendable. And yet so many of us still run our corporations as though they were farms tilled by poor peasants or construction sites populated by beasts of burden masquerading as humans. If you still run your organization like that, its demise is not in question; only the time of death is.

We simply cannot continue to run corporations with "Big Men" at the helm who take all the rewards and perks, and lots of employees who earn no more than their daily bread and who offer no more than the minimum effort. The era in which all we need are mute replaceable androids is long gone—it just hasn't left our management practices yet. In the knowledge economy, we need bright ideas and passionate people all around us, at all levels.

Competing to win, however, will not be done on the basis of the low-cost advantage that such corporate dictatorships are organized to achieve. We need to develop products that have winning features, customer experiences that are memorable and brands that connect and resonate. And we are not going to deliver those things with armies of disgruntled, barely awake employees.

So how do we get humans to do the work of humans?

Once you appreciate that you employ a human being and not a human resource, you start to appreciate certain insights: that people do their best work when they feel involved and connected, that they bring their best side to work when they feel appreciated and rewarded, and that their primary motivators are intrinsic: a feeling of control; of personal growth; of involvement in a cause. Contrary to the beliefs of some, these motivators need to act on every employee in the organization, from the cleaner upwards. They are not the preserve of the top cadre.

As more and more people leave the poverty line behind, we need to smarten up our views on management and leadership. Too many have viewed management as the exercising of power and control over the many by the few; too few have understood that it is more the development of a talented, engaged, purposeful collective force. It may take time, but the organizations who grasp this difference early will win in the long run.

The rest? They will find that they lose customers because their employees couldn't care less about serving them, that they can't produce quality because no one in the company really cares about it, that even their star employees are mere mercenaries looking for the better pay package, and that half the workforce is moonlighting using company resources.

Lazy leaders will still reduce the employment contract to an obligation to exchange money for labour. The enlightened ones will do the harder work: of enrolling the hearts and minds of employees in a common mission, and of spending time coaching and mentoring people to succeed, rather than waiting for them to fail and be replaced.

It is time to understand the being behind the human, not just the resource standing in front of you. The best work happens when employees earn a life, not just a living.

The Invisible Boss

Imagine that you can turn yourself invisible. Imagine also that you possess an "engagement meter": a tiny device that you can point at people and that shoots invisible laser beams that measure their degree of engagement with the task they're doing. The number shows up discreetly on the device in your hand: "1" for people who are utterly disengaged and don't care; "10" for those happy folks who love what they are doing with a great passion and want to do it better and better.

Imagine that your invisible self walks over to your most disengaged employee. You know, Fred, sitting in

> **It is time to understand the being behind the human,** not just the resource standing in front of you.

the corner there, who never seems to have anything to contribute, who looks bored and detached all the time, who complains bitterly after every pay appraisal. There he is, slumped at his desk, playing a soccer game on his computer.

It's five o'clock on a Friday. Your worst employee makes a beeline for the door, and your invisible self follows closely. You intend to spend the whole weekend shadowing this person and using your engagement meter on him.

What do you think you will find? You expect, of course, to discover that Fred is an inveterate cynic. That he hates everything and everyone, and is just lazy and work-shy by nature. But what will you actually find? I submit that most people on this planet are not hardened gloom merchants. They have a light inside them, but they just aren't given a place where they can let it shine out.

I submit further that as you follow Fred around invisibly, zapping him with your (painless) engagement meter, you will discover that the device gives him high readings at various possible points in the weekend:

- If Fred is recently in an intimate relationship, when he is having dinner with his companion on Friday evening
- If Fred is a devoted father, when he is playing with his children on Saturday morning

- If Fred is a sports fan, when he is watching his favourite team with his friends at the bar on Saturday afternoon
- If Fred is religious, when he is at his place of worship on Sunday morning, singing hymns with great gusto
- If Fred is a bibliophile, when he is curled up with a novel on Sunday afternoon
- If Fred is a fitness enthusiast, when he is pumping iron at the gym early on Monday morning before coming back to work.

I venture that Fred is going to give you very good readings on that little gadget of yours at various junctures—perhaps even scores of 8 or 9 out of 10.

The fact remains, however, that you will struggle to get even an engagement level of 4 out of 10 from Fred at your workplace. So whose fault is that: Fred's—or yours?

The essential problem is this: Fred does not come to work to earn a life; he just comes to earn a living. He comes only to earn his daily bread. And daily bread is all he earns.

Fred (and Fiona and Farhana and Femi and as many as eight out of every ten workers on the planet) are not really gaining any intrinsic pleasure from their work. They do it only to get a paycheck at the end of the month. The paycheck is the thing: it pays the bills, puts food on the table, allows for a bit of enjoyment of life.

That enjoyment, note, does not really happen at the place of work. Indeed, it's not even supposed to happen there. Most workplaces, even in the twenty-first century, are not set up for enjoyment. Most managers and supervisors would have a fit if they thought their colleagues were, heaven forbid, having fun as they worked. And yet, in the standout organizations on this planet, many people are thoroughly engaged with their work. They wear the brand on their chest, proudly. They wake up excited to do something of meaning with their day. They feel good about their personal growth. They look forward to working with invigorating colleagues.

That is exactly as it should be. Work should be a very big deal, not the tiny one most of us seem to make it. Work is integral to a good life, to our sense of meaning. A great life is one in which great work was done, work that benefited others. No one will remember you for your leisure hours.

As Though People Mattered

What's the most common thing you hear political and business leaders say when strife or carnage happens in their country? That it's having a bad effect on the economy. That economic purchasing power is heading south. That the investment climate is suffering.

What's wrong with this picture? All of the above is true, but does it really capture the essential point? We should indeed be worried about the financial impact of what happens in our world, but is that really all there is to worry about?

Here's a crazy thought for you: insecurity in the world is first and foremost a major problem because our people are dying and suffering, not because businesses are affected.

Many years ago, E. F. Schumacher published a thought-provoking little book: *Small Is Beautiful: Economics As If People Mattered.* The "people mattered" part of that is really important. I studied economics myself, and it was never because I wanted to learn how to use equations to maximize profit. It was because I wanted to understand the welfare of the human collective, and what systems and philosophies can optimize the wellbeing of people. People. Not abstract entities or organizations or nations. Schumacher warned that if we elevate goods above people, and consumption above creative activity, we will limit what it means to be human. And guess what—we did exactly that.

Have you ever asked yourself why our practice of business and economics is so far removed from what we are taught in our spiritual traditions, or even from what we know to be true in our normal lives as human beings? Why are we so preoccupied with accounting abstractions like GDP and EBITDA, but not the human beings that create them?

The extreme of that approach is visible in many societies today. Work is done primarily to benefit others, so it is viewed as a chore, a necessary evil, something to be avoided. Humans are viewed as resources, so the aim is to wring every drop of work out of them whilst pretending to motivate them. Because society is structured for the privileged few, the majority lead lives of futility and frustration. The worker tries to dodge work; the employer tries to replace workers with machines and looks forward to the day when robots and software can be deployed instead of humans.

Even more chillingly, a few deaths, or even a lot, are not really a big deal. The little people die all the time—in road crashes, in acts of thuggery, in the attacks of terrorists, or through the deeds of those who sell them dangerous alcohol or fake medicines. It's OK. It's all just road kill, collateral damage. As long as the big people are safe. That's why we have heavily armed guards protecting the well-to-do, but we can barely muster a response when it's the little folk being slaughtered.

The sooner we realize that this is not a natural state of being, the better for all of us. It is not natural to have to live behind razor wires and security alarms for fear of your fellow man; it is not natural to worry that should you have an accident on a highway the first thing that people running to the scene are likely to do is rob you.

Schumacher pointed out very eloquently that this situation is not sustainable. Slowly but surely, the social fabric erodes, people get engaged in a me-first struggle for survival, fights for land and resources erupt everywhere and the environment is destroyed for narrow personal gain. Sound familiar?

So how would we do things differently? How would we run the world—our nations and our corporations—as though people mattered? It can be done, and is being done. Henry Hazlitt showed us how, way back in 1946:

> The art of economics consists in looking not merely at the immediate but at the longer effects of any act or policy; it consists in tracing the consequences of that policy not merely for one group but for all groups.

Read it again. Hazlitt gives us a simple rule for deciding whether a policy or act is worthwhile: does it have a positive impact on as many groups as possible in the economy (not just one group), and will its effects stay positive in the long term (not just immediately)?

What if governments made policy decisions using this golden rule? Anything aimed unsustainably at a small clique would be ruled out. Some projects might pass muster on the first half of the rule (that it is aimed at the many rather than the few), but most would struggle with the second half (whether the project sounds at all sustainable or will just fizzle out after tenders are signed).

Think about what successive governments have done across the world. Have they really worked for all the people, and for the long term? Quite the opposite: so many expenditures over the years have benefited very narrow interest groups, and few initiatives have brought lasting benefits. Many African nations, for example, face widespread starvation or even famine every few years, decades after gaining their independence. Why? Because the entitlements to food are not widely spread. They have forgotten to look after the many, not just the few, and they do nothing for the long term—they just raise money for emergency food year after year. Hazlitt's golden rule is ignored completely.

We're good at criticizing government, but what about the way we run our organizations? Do we really organize them as though people matter? CEOs are very good at trumpeting "our people are our greatest asset" and "our business is centred on customers," but is there any real truth there? Why, then, are staff tossed out in every downturn and customers gouged in the absence of meaningful competition?

Way too many companies are just vehicles for maximizing the returns to principal shareholders and senior executives, period. Customers are the suckers tricked into supplying the money; employees are the resources deployed to provide the labour. The real rewards accrue upstairs.

A great business doesn't look anything like that. A great business follows the golden rule: it does things for the greater good of as many people as possible, and it

**A business should
be an ecosystem**
that aims to keep many
elements in harmony.

aims to stick around for centuries, not just a few explosive years. In fact, modern business leaders should learn a great deal from nature. A business should be an ecosystem that aims to keep many elements in harmony. Imbalance in the shared value system causes the entire setup to collapse, eventually.

We have forgotten a central fact of life: human endeavour is about people, not numbers. It is about enrolling citizens and employees in a collective purpose, in which they participate with enthusiasm and shared meaning. It is not just about selling to customers, but also about bonding with them in a shared belief system. It is about spreading rewards and leaving no one behind. Sadly, that's not how most of the world works today. We only sing these noble things in churches and temples and at corporate events, but we walk out ready to maximize personal gain in the shortest time possible, whatever it takes.

So if you wonder why we can't save our trees and elephants, or why we can't deal with insecurity and terrorism, wonder no longer. It's because we are not focused on the greater good for the greater time. It's why we have angry and frustrated masses everywhere, and why the elite are increasingly jittery and scared. We break the golden rule at our peril.

The Outstanding Employee

Because employers never consider the golden rule, most employees feel disillusioned and disenchanted. Too many feel stuck in dead-end jobs with no prospect of growth or advancement. Too many are stagnating on the chair they sit on, petrifying their careers instead of electrifying them. Most employees feel little sense of purpose in their work and are mostly disengaged from the brand and mission of their employers.

This is fundamentally a failure of leadership and management. However, let's take a different perspective this time. What's wrong with the employees themselves? Why do so many allow themselves to become sullen and unresponsive, thereby killing their own advancement?

There is also another breed of worker, remember: the folks who are always full of energy and enthusiasm, always ready to do a bit more than duty calls for, ever willing to go the extra mile. Why is it that such people exist, even in the very same dreary, poorly led organizations that seem to sap the life-force out of most other workers? What makes these people different?

If you're an employee with ambitions, allow me to let you in on something at this point. I interact with many leaders and employers in different ways, and I know that there are certain attributes that mark out their "star" workers. Those staffers who demonstrate these traits are usually the ones who are most valued, given greater responsibility and selected for promotion. There are four characteristics that stand out. Let's consider them in turn.

The first such attribute is *taking responsibility*. The person who takes charge of situations and handles them; who takes over the burden of accountability; who gets things done without needing to always seek validation—what boss would not value such an employee?

The second attribute is *anticipation*. The employee who can see problems before they occur, and can defuse them before they grow, is rare indeed. The person who takes the burden of anticipation off the boss and who prevents a crisis is always valued.

Thirdly, leaders go for people they can *trust*. People of integrity and an inbuilt sense of ethics are increasingly rare and increasingly sought after. Even leaders who are not trustworthy themselves are always looking for juniors they can trust! No employer wants to give responsibility to a rogue who might defraud her, after all.

Lastly, leaders rate those employees who exhibit high levels of *positive personal energy*. Enthusiasm is infectious—but so is apathy. It is very hard to keep energy levels high in most organizations, and those employees who have great reservoirs of zest are always very useful. The zest need not be externally visible, please note; this is not about everyone exhibiting manic extroversion. Personal energy can be hidden inside the individual and yet create excellent results.

So there you have it: employees who take their jobs seriously, who solve problems rather than observe them, who can be left in charge of serious stuff and who buzz around every day regardless of circumstances—those are the people who get rated highly by employers. If you're a person of substance who wants to go places, don't just sit back pessimistically. Put yourself in work's way. Take charge of situations; show initiative. Give a damn about what's going on. Solve problems when they occur and, better still, before they occur. Be cheerful, and show it. Protect the business like it's your own, even though it isn't.

A bigger deal awaits, even in employment. Make these traits your own, and things will happen for you, no matter how bad your current employer is. You are what you repeatedly do. Good habits become lifelong traits. Even if you outgrow your current boss and place of work, the habits will help you thrive wherever you go. Someday, the four habits will be applied in the correct arena: an enlightened organization that rewards you for them, or even your own business where you deploy them for personal gain. But the time to start working on them is right now—and they won't let you down.

So don't join the crowd of fatalists. Rise above your current circumstances, and soon your circumstances will catch up.

Rise above your current circumstances, and soon your circumstances will catch up.

The Taxi Driver and the Shop Assistants

During a recent holiday, I took a taxi from the hotel where I was staying to visit a nearby shopping mall. The driver was courteous and polite. He maintained a very clean and pleasing vehicle. He was solicitous and considerate and did everything possible for his customer's convenience, such as driving carefully, maintaining a good air-conditioning system in a very hot climate and keeping some newspapers and sightseeing brochures in his car as reading material.

I then arrived at a certain shop specializing in high-end clothing at the mall. Two shop assistants were seated at the desk. Both were busy chatting loudly and animatedly about what was evidently an intensely personal matter. Neither looked up, even to make eye contact. I looked around the shop; it had some good brands and decent merchandise. I wondered about sizes, but neither "assistant" interrupted the flow of chatter to come over to offer "assistance." I decided not to support this particular venture, and left. The shop was, in any case, empty of customers. And for good reason.

The taxi driver was alert, and signalled when he saw me returning. He had parked the car under a tree and opened all the windows to keep it cool. After we arrived back at the hotel, he offered me a business card, which I made sure I kept safe for the future. The shop, on the other hand, is not one I will visit again.

So what's the difference between the taxi driver and the shop assistants? First, the obvious one: the taxi driver runs his own business; the shop assistants don't. The taxi driver has "skin in the game": he earns or burns on the decisions he makes. If he conducts a good business and puts in the hard work and maintains high standards, his children get to eat well and go to school. A few days' lost business, on the other hand, can be catastrophic. The shop assistants, meanwhile, are reluctant recruits in someone else's business dream. They don't feel any immediate pain or gain from what they do on a given day. It takes a while for their behaviour to translate into personal consequences, if at all.

So was the lesson of my little outing that people who own businesses are more motivated than those who don't? Well, sort of. Human life is ruled by incentives, after all. But that alone is too simple an argument. We have all sat in taxis that are decrepit and dirty and are driven by lifelong sourpusses. Equally, we have all encountered shop assistants who are perky, helpful and cheerful at all times, despite the fact that they are working for others for meagre pay.

I would venture further to say that the taxi driver I encountered on that day would do a good job even if he took the place of those shop assistants. And that those two employees would make a thorough hash of any business, if they ever found the gumption to open one.

How we react to the world and situation around us is very much a personal deal. If we have high standards,

> **How we react to the world and situation around us is very much a personal deal.** If we have high standards, we tend to have them in whatever we put our mind to doing.

we tend to have them in whatever we put our mind to doing. If we are lazy and whiny about life, we tend to bring that behaviour to everything.

This is something that thoughtful business owners need to consider very carefully. Those uninterested folks you leave to run your businesses on their own? They can bring it to its knees, simply by not giving a damn. You have to select your people very carefully and introduce some serious incentives to perform—not just pecuniary rewards, but the harder stuff: a sense of belonging, and a feeling of participation in a deal bigger than mere employment.

Now that stuff is tough. Which is why so many of our establishments remain populated with couldn't-care-less employees. Is yours? If so, a leader has failed somewhere. Most do.

Let the Whole Human Being Come to Work

Management thinker Bob Sutton wrote in 2012 on his blog about an incident involving a friend's young daughter, Phoebe. The ten-year-old girl had been booked to fly unaccompanied on a well-known airline—for an additional charge.

If you know big organizations, you know what happened next. No one showed up to help Phoebe make her complicated transfer, so she missed her connection.

She asked airline employees for help over and over—to no avail. They were too busy. The girl's frantic parents, on discovering their little girl had not showed up at the final destination, called the airline repeatedly. Also to no avail. All that employees could say was that unaccompanied minor service was outsourced, and hence not their problem.

Did this tale have a happy ending? Only when Phoebe's father was talking to an airline employee and asking her to please find his daughter. The response? The employee said she was about to end her shift, so she couldn't help. Phoebe's dad then asked the woman if she was a mother herself, and what if it were her child missing... That did the trick. The girl was found in just fifteen minutes.

What's happening here? Is this airline a particularly bad organization? It features repeatedly in social-media exposés, but that's not the point. Most large organizations (and many small ones too) are exactly like this—because they are designed to be.

The point is this: in most employment, you're supposed to leave your humanity at the door and become an employee, dude. The airline staff were not being inhuman, they were doing their jobs, as defined by their bosses and standard operating procedures. Compared to moving huge planes and thousands of passengers around the country, the plight of a lost little girl did not feature on the radar. Humans who are being human help other people. The staffer who finally helped find Phoebe did so once she thought like a mother and not like an employee.

What a shameful waste of life, to be employing like that and be employed like that. And what a waste of talent. This type of culture of employment is a throwback to feudal times and factory models, when we really wanted robots and automatons but were forced to employ thinking, feeling humans. Such a model has no place in modern society, and we should hang our heads in shame that we allow it to persist.

I repeat: the whole human being comes to work, not just the employee bit. The idea that people should become unfeeling androids when they are employed is a ridiculous pretence. In many companies, being inhuman is even termed "professionalism," as though it's something to be celebrated.

If you're an employer: embrace the entire human being before you. Understand your employees like humans understand other humans, not like slave-drivers viewing "human resources" on the cotton fields of the past. Celebrate people as people and you'll get the best out of them. If you want employees not to have feelings, unfeeling work is all you'll get, and, eventually, a workforce consisting mostly of actual robots.

If you're an employee: don't sit there waiting for an excellent employer to appear in your life or for great work to fall into your lap. It doesn't work like that. Do your best work in all your work, and soon the habit of excellence will take root. That habit—which entails giving things your best shot, fixing things before complaining about them, and taking responsibility for your own motivation—is what propels people to achieving their bigger deals. People who are engrossed in their work and take it very seriously are the ones who become invaluable to others.

Work to earn a life. The living will take care of itself.

4

Religions Get It. Sports Teams Get It. **Do You?**

When people are financially invested, they want a return. When people are emotionally invested, they want to contribute.

SIMON SINEK

WHERE WE START
TO MAKE THE WORKPLACE
FIT FOR **HUMAN
BEINGS,** NOT JUST
HUMAN RESOURCES.

The Meaning of Meaning at Work

What is to be done? How do we make a bigger deal of the workplace?

Before we answer that question, ask yourself this: whose brand do your employees feel more connected to—yours, or the brand of a football team, a church, a type of apparel or a mobile phone? The sad fact is that most of your people probably feel more bonding to some faraway sports team that they never see in person, to a religious organization to which they willingly give a tenth of their income every month or to the brand of the phone or sneakers that they so ostentatiously sport every day. In which case those organizations have extracted genuine engagement from your people, while yours hasn't.

Bizarre, isn't it? You provide your employee with a livelihood, you help put her children through college, you stock her refrigerator with food, you allow her to buy good clothes, and yet she reserves her passion and loyalty for other people's organizations. How painful is that?

Look beyond the pain and discern what is going on here. Those other organizations have your employee's attention and loyalty because they bestow meaning to her life. The employer generally doesn't. The employer just exchanges labour for payment. The employer-employee relationship is too often merely transactional, not emotional.

Let's break it down. Where do we find meaning in work? I am indebted to Gurnek Bains and his co-authors for their book *Meaning Inc.* and their early work in deciphering what meaning in the workplace might look like. Their essential insight was that we experience meaning when what we are doing is connected to something else, something bigger. When our work feels part of something significant and something that matters to us, we encounter meaning. When our work gives us relevance or context, we feel part of a bigger deal. And that's when we do our best work.

So how do we bring meaning to the workplace? By connecting the work that employees do with the things that matter to them. What things matter to human beings? Feeling involved and appreciated, and making

When our work gives us relevance or context, we feel part of a bigger deal. **And that's when we do our best work.**

an impact in life. More specifically, here is my version
of the sentiments that make employees feel they are
bonded with their organizations:

1. **I am growing and developing:** Every person needs to
   feel a sense of meaningful advancement in life. None
   of us wants to experience the desperation of being
   stuck in a rut. When people feel they are accessing and
   developing their unique, personal strengths, they feel
   forward movement. An organization must offer this
   feeling of psychological growth, of mastery of a particular skill set. The nature of growth can vary—not
   everyone is destined to rise to the C-suite, after all—
   but every employee must feel the opportunity exists
   to get better and better at something they like doing.

2. **I am getting my just rewards:** We say it all the time,
   do we not: money isn't everything. And truly, it is not.
   Anyone who spent even a little time thinking about the
   rewards that money brings to a life would conclude that
   they are ephemeral at best. None of us wants to create
   an organization that runs only on monetary reward, a
   transactional sweatshop populated by mercenaries all
   the way to the top. And yet, we can't forget the other
   part: money can't be everything, but it certainly needs
   to be something. I tell all my clients to take everyone's
   attention off the money issue. If money stays a problem, that's all you'll ever talk about. Specifically, pay as

much as you can afford, not as little as you can get away with. And most importantly, work to make your compensation system as fair as humanly possible. Human beings react very harshly to perceived unfairness. They want to feel everyone is given a fair shake and that the game is not rigged against them. This requires both sincerity in leaders and transparency in the system.

3. **I feel like I belong here:** The human being yearns to belong, to feel part of something bigger. We get that feeling from our religions, our communities, our ideologies, our hobbies—but do we ever get it from our employers? Quite the opposite: most organizations, after decades of brutal restructurings and desultory layoffs, suffer from very low trust levels. Yet those few organizations that create a genuine sense of belonging—the feeling that "this is your home; stay here with us"—are mostly the very ones that get unusual performance out of people.

4. **My life has invigorating purpose:** As Simon Sinek has pointed out (in his excellent book *Start With Why* and in a much-watched TED Talk), most organizations are adept at spelling out the *what, how, who, where* and *when* of everything—but terrible at explaining, or even having, the *why*. "Why is this important?" is the most important motivator of all. We feel less like specks on a speck when we feel part of a bigger deal or are given

a role in a larger movement. But think about it: when was the last time a boss (convincingly) told you *why* what you do is so important?

5. **I connect with the history and values here:** People don't just want to know their role in the future; they also want to feel their connection to a valued past. Many humans give their best when they feel part of an honoured tradition, a link in a continuing chain. As Bains et al. put it, "People almost universally feel that their work activities lack coherence. Many feel they are disembodied actors in a swirling change drama that has no beginning, middle or end." Great leaders always give a sense of history, not just a sense of future. It is important for all of us to feel that we are a continuation of something important that has gone on before.

6. **I believe in this brand and am proud to be part of it:** External perceptions are very important to the human being. What we think of ourselves is shaped heavily by what we think others think of us. As a result, being part of a respected or loved brand is a powerful driver of meaning at work. I always ask CEOs: Do your staff wear your branded merchandise with pride, or only because they are made to? Do they sport your logo on weekends, because they want others to know where they work? Or do they hope no one asks that question?

7. **My personal impact is clear—to me and to everyone else:** Much as the bigger picture in which we fit is important to us, at the end of the day we don't want to just be anonymous, unnoticed, unappreciated cogs in a machine. We want to feel that our own activities also matter. An organization that understands this tries very hard to value and highlight every person's contribution, no matter how mundane. People need to feel that what they do is important, makes a difference and is valued by others.

You will never be able to make all your employees feel all these things all of the time. No one can pull that off. But look around your workplace: are you even managing to bestow some of those feelings on most of the people most of the time? Because that's what it takes to make a bigger deal of the workplace.

In Service of a Bigger Deal

Is this bigger-deal thing done by any organization at all, though?

In my observation, two types of organization regularly pull off the bigger deal in giving meaning to their people—the first for millennia; the second for decades. I'm referring to religious organizations and sports teams. Look at the list of seven connectors I just described, and you will see that those sorts of organizations are very good at creating intangible connections with their fans and followers and employees. They create a sense of belonging and involvement, belief in the brand and connection to a higher purpose, to great effect. So much so that the issues of personal reward and personal impact are largely subsumed.

The world's greatest sporting franchises last for a century or more, the world's enduring religious organizations for millennia. Yet the average business organization struggles to make it past even a few years of success. The key difference? One side is creating an enduring cause in the hearts and minds of its people; the other is just creating a set of transactions.

How do religions do it? They use some of the connectors to great effect. They give people a powerful sense of purpose, of course, but they also connect people to a shared history; they create a brand that people are proud to wear, even to promote and spread; they give followers a powerful sense of belonging; and they often give ordinary people work to do in the community, work that feels important and valued, in the service of a higher ideal. They follow rituals and regular practice that create a rhythm in the lives of their followers. Religions do these things so well that the issue of "compensation" does not come up, at least not in an earthly sense; people give of their time and money freely and wait for their rewards in another life.

What about sports teams? As with religions, the vast majority of their stakeholders are neither employees nor customers in the traditional sense, but fans—willing, enthusiastic followers. They are willing to work for the team if asked; they are willing to fund it; they are willing to buy anything associated with the team. Dedicated sports fans follow the vicissitudes of their teams' fortunes as though the ups and downs are happening to their own families—which in a sense they are. The sense of belonging being created is that powerful, and most of it is propagated by the fans themselves; no HR or PR department needed. And yet many sports fans live thousands of miles away from their team—they will probably never actually visit the stadium or meet the players. But that is no obstacle. The manic connection continues regardless.

What's actually happening here? Religions and sports teams excel at myth-making: creating meaning and motivation through the power of shared narrative. In *Sapiens*, his remarkable sweep through human history, Yuval Noah Harari highlights the potency of common myth. Indeed, he posits that the creation of powerful shared narratives is what has made humans stand out from other animals: we have managed to create corporations, nations and empires precisely because we have the power to create stories—and believe them. Religions and sports teams are especially adept at this. They create storylines, legends and iconic figures so well that the humans who become believers don't even have to be present in the same location or ever meet in their lifetimes. And remember, these organizations were doing this long before global communication was ever possible.

I don't mean to suggest that the stories are lies. Every religion emerges from an actual event in history; every great sports team does indeed have measured and recorded accomplishments. What is remarkable, however, is that these institutions go from local to global so quickly by crafting a story that traverses the world and enrols new believers in every fresh generation. The issue here is not whether you or I believe the story, but the power of shared narrative: human beings need to feel they are part of a bigger picture, that they have a role on a stage that matters to them.

Working humans spend more time at work than doing pretty much anything else in their lives. So why is it that corporations are some of the least effective at creating meaningful shared narrative? Precisely because most businesses are run by small dealers: people whose primary interest is short-term self-gain and who view their "followers" as resources to be exploited, not fellow voyagers on a quest. Certainly, many business leaders have picked up on this gap. They try to craft mission statements and values that purport to ennoble their enterprises. But, as Chapter 6 of this book will show, these are most often empty words, and their emptiness is apparent even as they are uttered. That's not a shared narrative or a belief system—that's mere posturing.

It's true that corporations would struggle to replicate the fervent zeal and remarkable emotional connections that churches and sports organizations can engender. Nonetheless, they should take a closer look at what is going on with the believers and supporters of these special setups. Can we really not put a few drops of this powerful potion in our enterprises? Why is it a given that the average person's work in a company should be meaningless—short-lived, unemotional, uncaring?

Go and look at the faces of your employees when they are singing in church or when there are five minutes to go in a cup final and ask yourself, "Are these the same people who work for me? What makes the big difference in their sense of connection to that organization as opposed to mine?" The big dealer sees this difference very clearly, feels it acutely and does something about it. The small dealer whines about "work being different" and sticks to the tired old equation: dollars earned for hours of time sacrificed.

Fit for Human Beings

Let's get practical now. What can you do to make your workplace fit for human beings, not human resources?

Go and look at the faces of your employees when they are singing in church or when there are five minutes to go in a cup final and ask yourself, **'Are these the same people who work for me?'**

How do we find those few drops of the potion that religious and sporting organizations seem to have in abundance? The following six suggestions are based on my own observations of workplaces over three decades.

1. **Get the issue of money off the table:** Stop making every conversation you have with your employees about money. Pay well: competitively, fairly, as generously as you can. Don't pay the minimum you can get away with; pay the maximum you can sensibly afford. Your reward will arrive in the years to come—when you are perceived to be a good employer who isn't stingy on pay, who attracts good people, whose people go the extra mile and whose customers encounter smiling staff. Offset those benefits against the additional salary costs and you may find a very different equation to ponder.

2. **Involve your people in key decisions:** Nothing shouts "resource" louder to an employee than a boss who just issues instructions (or worse, barks them). If you are the genius who gets it all, and all you need are people to execute your orders mindlessly, then mindless is all you'll get. Practice listening. Ask every member of a team their opinion before you pronounce any verdicts. Pay attention; weave strands of diverse thought together; conclude and validate. You'll still be leading, make no mistake: there's a common misconception

that leadership is just about brute conviction and force of personality. It's not. Nor is a business a democracy where everyone has a say. A wise leader, however, is a listening leader. Such a leader's employees feel their views are welcome and are heard before decisions are made. When you become a listening, integrating leader, you'll finally be leading your people into a bigger deal.

3. **Have honest conversations:** If the bosses always keep their cards close to their chest, if they always display an insincere face to their people, if they engage in sudden surprises like layoffs, if they talk to employees as though they're doing a PR spiel for the media, then, surprise surprise, the employees will respond in kind. If insincerity is the modus operandi, then insincerity will rule. Everyone will wear a mask and have an unseen agenda. Far better to share problems, give honest feedback and ask for it, and sort out issues together. That way, even when tough decisions have to be made, they are made in the open where they can be seen and appreciated.

4. **Use celebrations, rituals and symbols:** What do sports teams and churches do so well that corporations don't? Create shared history and collective ambition. One of the ways to do that is to have celebration days in the calendar; to observe regular rituals like appreciation of good performance, or "podium moments" when the

organization achieves something meaningful; and to create feel-good symbols of belonging that are given out freely to staff. If you want to make connections on intangibles, the path there is surprisingly full of tangibles: calendar entries, gifts and giveaways, joint celebrations and badges of identity.

5. **Offer genuine personal growth:** Don't just make noble statements about this one; bake it into your people system. The human being looks to the future, naturally. People respond when they can see a path for themselves, a path that leads to something better. Try to offer each person opportunities to become better at what they do or to try different things. It is not possible to promote or develop everyone, but it is perfectly possible to be willing to try. When I can't offer an employee any more growth, I do my best to get it for her somewhere else. Our biggest problem is in the appreciation that people need growth, not in the execution. The "career paths" we end up offering come across as insincere and illusory. If few believe in them, few will take them.

6. **Remember the little things:** If you're going to deal with human beings, you have to deal with the little things. Sure, humans need the big stuff: a sense of purpose and belonging; participation in a noble cause. But more often than not, our acceptance of the big stuff hinges

on our experience of the little stuff. We respond most warmly when we experience warmth; we extend courtesy when courtesy is extended to us. That is why a great business leader never forgets the basics: saying "please," "thanks" and "sorry" often, and meaning them. Never forget you are taking someone's time and effort, and you must be grateful for this. Never forget you are often stretching people beyond normal limits, and you must be remorseful about this. Cultivate an environment where humans work like humans, not like automatons: where people celebrate together, mourn together, laugh together.

" Cultivate an environment where humans work like humans, not like automatons: where people **celebrate together, mourn together, laugh together.** "

5

Create Value
for Others

"

You can have everything in life you want if you will just help enough other people get what they want."

ZIG ZIGLAR

WHERE WE LEARN TO
EXTRACT OURSELVES
FROM OURSELVES.

ALAIN DE BOTTON is, ostensibly, a philosopher. But the focus of his work is not abstruse concepts, but the practical realities of life. He also keeps up a barrage of thoughtful tweets. One of those tweets is the reason he's on this page today.

Here it is: "Behind almost every inconvenience is a new business waiting to be born."

One of the things I'm often told by young people seeking success is this: "I'm a born entrepreneur. I'm not cut out to be employed; I want to do my own thing. All I need is a viable business idea."

First things first: the true entrepreneurs don't ask anyone for business ideas—they know exactly where to find them. And so, it seems, does Mr. de Botton.

One of the runaway business product successes of recent times is M-Pesa, Kenya's trailblazing payments system that sends money via text messages on mobile phones. It is such an astonishing hit that it has changed the face of payments in Kenya and claims to channel a good chunk of the country's GDP every day. It has even changed the idea of what a bank is.

But why was it such a huge hit? The answer lies in the world before M-Pesa. How did you transfer money in the bad old days? Why, by having a bank account. Which entailed numerous visits to banks and endless interrogations and provisions of proof that you were indeed worthy of operating such a service. In Kenya, for the few who got an account, the transfer of money to others then involved more form-filling, signatures, delays and hefty fees. If you didn't qualify for an account, you stuffed some bank notes into a brown envelope, gave it to someone travelling by bus to pass on to your relatives and prayed hard that it arrived intact.

That is the series of huge inconveniences solved by M-Pesa. Suddenly, money could be transferred by a few clicks on the cheapest phone. Once Kenyans realized that the money so transferred did indeed arrive at the other end, the uptake was phenomenal. So it is with almost every big product success in history. It was big because the inconvenience it killed was big.

Which inconvenience did the television set kill? That of leaving your home for visual entertainment. The digital camera? Think of how you used to take photos in the film era—the cost, the many steps, the

unreliable results, the difficulty of sharing the outputs—
and you can see that the move to digital was inevitable.
The smartphone? It killed the idea that computing was
something that could only be done sitting tethered to
a desk working on a large, expensive, difficult-to-use
machine. The uptake figures of the cheaper, portable,
more usable alternative are another phenomenon.

And so all the business ideas you need are hidden
in plain sight, all around you. It's just that they aren't
in the shape of "products," but are visible today only
as "inconveniences." If you're serious about entre-
preneurship, get serious about life around you. Stay
curious and inquisitive. Observe ordinary people in their
ordinary lives, and see what annoys and vexes them
the most. Your success comes from solving problems
for others.

If you have your eyes open, you might see some
of the following in whichever urban area you live: the
impossibility of getting anything done that involves
moving around in soul-sapping traffic; the paucity of
dignified public-transport options; the fear of insecurity around every corner; the time squandered standing
pointlessly in lines everywhere; the unreliability of
artisans and technicians; the growing pollution that
blights the atmosphere.

Might I venture that there are enough future products
hidden in even that short list to power a future economy? So don't look for ideas; look for inconveniences.

Think about the World
You're Serving, Not Yourself

The human being is fixated on itself. Since we perceive life only through our own consciousness, we place ourselves at the centre of our existence. And we spend our lives fretting about our own selves: what we have and don't have; what we need and want; what we feel entitled to; what we should and could and would be doing, if only... The paradox is this: If you want to succeed, stop thinking about you. Start somewhere else.

Here's a simple example. Suppose you want to succeed by making and selling cakes. Here is a set of questions you will probably ask yourself: Do I have the skill to make cakes? Do I have the equipment and facilities? Do I have the capital to put into this little business? Will I be able to find customers? Do I have the guts to do this?

Legitimate questions, all. If you can answer most of them in the affirmative, you might actually go ahead and launch your cake business in January. And it will probably fail before December.

Why so? Because you started in the wrong place. Don't start with yourself; start with the world. The first question to ask is, does the world need more cakes? The answer to that is probably not. Before you move on to something else, though, go deeper. What's the problem here? There are many, many cakes being produced for the world, but what is not being supplied?

Is it a price problem? Could someone producing really affordable cakes open up a whole new market? Is it a taste problem? Does one cake taste pretty much like the next one? Could someone who revolutionizes the taste of cakes charge a premium for exclusivity? Is it a problem of homogeneity? Do cakes just look the same, wherever and whenever you eat them? Might someone who customizes cakes for special occasions, themes them and makes them look and taste different add value that's missing? Is it a convenience problem? Is it too much bother to go out in traffic to buy a cake? Does getting a custom-made one take far too long? Could people choose and customize their cakes on their smartphone and have them delivered? Is it a health problem? Are cakes just bad for you, and do they need to be bad? Could finding a way to give people festive treats they can really enjoy without harming themselves be the real challenge?

To answer those questions, you have to think hard about the world you're trying to serve, not about yourself. You come back to yourself once you have thought about what the market needs or doesn't yet know it needs. Then the questions you ask yourself in the mirror become these: Am I really trying to sell cakes, or am I just looking for an easy way to make some money? Do I really care enough about cakes to make the best ones in the world? Could I change the way cakes are designed, made, sold and delivered? What would that take? Now you might be onto something.

Replace cakes with pretty much any product or service in the argument above. The reason most businesses fail is they start with the wrong set of questions. They fixate on what they are capable of doing, not what is actually needed. And because most people starting something new think in the exact same way, they end up making similar things that are sold in similar ways and are similarly unsuccessful. And so they make average returns and eventually none at all.

As with business, so with life. When we think about what we are going to do with ourselves, we start with what we think we know about ourselves. We list off our qualifications, our credentials and our experiences. Then we set out to deliver what we think we have to the world. Just like everyone else out there.

Here's what you should really think about when you think about your own success: not what you should get from the world, but what the world should get from you. To do it that way, you have to pay deep attention to what's out there, not what's inside you. You need more windows to the world, not more mirrors reflecting yourself. It is an abiding lesson of life: you succeed by creating value for others first, and then for yourself. Not the other way around. Your success is a byproduct of the success you give to the world.

So, then: who succeeds because of you? Who gets a more enjoyable, more meaningful, more productive, more fulfilling life because of you? Focus on those

" The reason most businesses fail is they **start with the wrong set of questions.** "

"

Your success is a byproduct of the **success you give to the world.**

"

people. Your true success will lie with them. And if your honest answer to the question is "no one," stop right there and rethink everything.

The Spirit of Enquiry

To understand the concept of success through service, you need to get out of yourself and really study the world that you seek to serve. You have to immerse yourself deeply in the lives of those you are making offerings to. The big dealer does not just say, "Here's what I have; take it." She asks, "What's missing in your life? What challenges do you face? What would make your life easier?" And then, "What can I do for you?"

The answers to these questions do not come easily. To really do something meaningful in the lives of customers or beneficiaries comes not from a single questionnaire; it comes from a life spent in the spirit of enquiry. You have to excavate the solutions, not merely discover them. It takes determination and repeated effort. To pull it off, you need to have a strong quality: curiosity about the world you want to make an impact in. You need to be in a state of wonder, always observing, always asking, always connecting. The people who make the most impact are, in my experience, always like this. Relentlessly curious.

The Unwritten Laws of Business is an odd little book.

It was first published many decades ago by W. J. King and was updated in 2005 by James G. Skakoon to give it wider scope and to appeal to those in management. It contains some gems of wisdom, and "Let's Go See" is one of them. This phrase recommends that you inculcate the habit of going to see for yourself, rather than waiting for things to be brought to your desk. It points out that management is not the art of arranging one's posterior behind a desk for the day, using phones, computers and dictation machines as the tools of work. It is a far more active occupation that involves being where the action really is, as often as possible.

Most of us miss this fundamental point about success. So many seem to imagine that the higher one gets in the echelons of leadership, the more desk-bound one must become. Interacting with staff at their workstations, meeting customers, strolling through the shop floor—all of that is for lowly minions, surely? The boss's work is different: it involves sitting at an impressive desk in an expansive office making decisions, using data brought to that desk entirely by others. Is it any surprise that so many institutions are in so woeful a state, when "hands-on" management is so rare?

This is no way to run organizations. The more enlightened type of manager says, "Let's Go See!" to most situations, knowing that there is no substitute for direct experience or observation. Rather than read market survey reports to figure out what customers want, this manager goes out to ask them personally. Rather than accept what the HR manager says about staff motivation, this leader goes out to shoot the breeze with employees every day.

It is also no way to run your life. The enlightened parent does not issue edicts to the children from the breakfast table, based on an outmoded view of their lives. The curious parent watches keenly to see how children live, work and interact these days. You cannot guide anyone without understanding their lives.

What's the One Thing the World Wants from You?

The Michelin star is a time-honoured guide to excellence in the restaurant business. Way back in the 1920s, the Michelin brothers recruited a team of mystery diners—or restaurant inspectors—to visit and review restaurants anonymously. In 1926, the *Michelin Guide* began to award stars for fine dining establishments, initially marking them only with a single star. Later, a hierarchy of zero, one, two and three stars was introduced. By 2017, the *Guide* was rating more than 40,000 establishments in 24 territories across three continents, and more than 30 million *Michelin Guides* had been sold worldwide.

Getting a Michelin star is no joke. It makes and breaks reputations. It is controversial. Those who get one face intense pressure never to lose it. Those who

"

The people who make
the most impact are
relentlessly curious.

"

don't have one strive obsessively to land it—and are often outraged when they are overlooked year after year.

Over the years the *Michelin Guide* has faced many accusations: of being too focused on French cooking as the supposed pinnacle of cuisine; of being in thrall to celebrity chefs; of ignoring simpler food. To stay relevant, the *Guide* has had to broaden its brief to embrace many more tastes. Japan now runs a close second to France in the total number of starred restaurants. But here's the surprise: the *Michelin Guide* has started recognizing even very humble enterprises. Ramen and dim sum restaurants in Hong Kong and Tokyo and popular hawker joints in Singapore have been awarded stars. These eateries serve food for just a few dollars, making them the cheapest Michelin-starred restaurants in the world.

Wait, can such basic mass-market enterprises be worthy of stars given to very refined chefs? Of course they can. It should come as no surprise. The only surprise is how long it took Michelin to get there. The *Guide* itself will tell you: "Stars are awarded to restaurants based on the quality of their food alone." All other things—service, ambience, et cetera—are secondary. And that is the truth of the matter. We'd like to go to restaurants for the full experience: friendly and efficient service, a great location or setting and beautiful decor. All of these matter; of course they do. But what is the one thing that a great restaurant must deliver?

Great-tasting food. If the food is just-there mediocre, no amount of service refinement or expensive furnishings make any difference. If your food isn't up to scratch, you don't have a great restaurant. Great food is the one thing every restaurant aspiring to greatness must deliver. The other elements of user experience are important add-ons, but they're not vital. That is why we have the phenomenon of hawker stalls winning Michelin stars. They are tiny, basic affairs and you have to queue up to get anything—but the food is to die for.

So if you want to start a seriously good restaurant, you have to focus on seriously good food. Without that, you just have a venue, not a restaurant. And so it is with other lines of business. What is the one thing a bank must have, without which it isn't a bank? Trust. No amount of fancy digital products or snazzy-looking branches or ever-smiling employees can help a bank where trust is broken. If you think your bank will misuse your money, it ceases to be a bank.

What is the one thing that an internet service provider must offer, above everything else? Reliability. The internet is nothing if it isn't always on. The fastest speeds are meaningless if they disappear from time to time. The best internet connection is invisible and unnoticed—it just allows you to get on with your life. In modern life the internet is like electricity or water. You have to have it, but you don't want to think about it. If it disappears even briefly, everyone in your home or office will scream blue murder. And yet ISP leaders are often preoccupied with marketing and pricing and packaging gimmicks rather than what should be the heart of their business: reliability.

What's the one thing for insurance companies? Faith that they will pay up when trouble strikes. For hotels building long-term relationships? Hospitality, in the original meaning of the word. For hospitals? Healing. For professional advisors? Their clients' success.

All these one things are the must-haves—the absolute essentials. You build your business around your one thing as the core. The nice-to-haves are layered on. They matter, but never as much as the one thing does. Without your one thing, you don't have a business. Do you know what yours is? The one thing that, if you don't get it right, means you don't really have a business, a profession, an offering? What's your "one thing" if you are a lawyer? A doctor? A spiritual guide? A parent? If you think deeply enough, you will see there is always a fundamental purpose in your work, something that is the core of what you do.

And yet, don't imagine that your one thing is the only thing. Your customer depends on your one thing and will leave you if you don't offer it all the time. But that doesn't mean that's all the customer wants. Customers are touchy and demanding people, and because they cover your company's payroll and bills and keep your children in good schools, they have every right to be!

If you're a bank, priority number one is to have the tightest possible governance and controls. Your customers must trust that their money is safe with you and that they can trust you to protect their futures. Once you have delivered that trust, remember that this one thing is necessary but not sufficient. No matter how much your customers trust you, they still demand branches that are close to them *and* a cutting-edge mobile app that means they don't have to visit branches.

The take-home is this: In business, figure out the must-have "one thing" your customers want from you. Deliver that one thing at all times, and protect its uniqueness. Then move outwards and add other features to provide an overall experience that customers value—while never forgetting your one thing.

Take that to your next strategy session.

Maintain, Maintain, Maintain

Let's say you studied the inconveniences around you and found one to kill in a unique way. Let's say you made "Let's Go See" your leadership mantra and uncovered great insights every day. Let's say you understood your business's "one thing" and made sure you delivered that one thing. Customers are delighted; the cash tills are ringing. Are you done, now—you've cracked it?

"

Without your one thing,
you don't have a business.
**Do you know what
yours is?**

"

Not quite. Now you have to protect your greatness.

One of my favourite local restaurants closed down recently. I don't have many favourites. In fact, I don't need more than the fingers of one hand to count them. So losing even one of them is a big deal. And yet it is so, so common.

The story usually goes like this: An unusually good eatery opens with a bang. The owner seems to have a very clear vision of the cuisine to be served and the style with which it is to be done. It has a focused menu of just a few dishes, not the mismatched mishmash of me-too fare so many try to offer. It has a colour-themed, tastefully done interior. An experienced and passionate chef has been brought in to design and deliver the menu. The staff are energetic and attentive. It all just works, in other words. Word spreads and the place begins filling up. It becomes a favourite for the foodies who know good food when they encounter it.

But, disturbingly often, the warning signs will begin to appear. The fittings will start to look worn, and no one will seem concerned. The waiting staff will change often, and the newcomers will look like they'd rather be doing something else with their lives. Most damningly, the dishes will begin to deteriorate. They will now look slapdash on the plate, and that magical taste will become elusive. Many dishes will often not be available, for no apparent reason. The original chef will have left without leaving any legacy and will usually not be replaced as juniors are asked to step up. The restaurant owner will now have more pressing business interests. And then it's gone.

What's the big deal, you might ask? Businesses close all the time—it's part of the game. The restaurant industry in particular is notoriously unstable. Most people who open restaurants end up closing them, too.

But wait. I get exasperated when this happens because many places I've seen in recent years have done all the hard work. They came up with a concept that works and draws patrons. They got the most important ingredient—the food—right. They turned out consistently excellent fare. They even got the people-side working, with a crew of highly motivated servers carrying the day, day after day. Having got their show on the road so well, and having overcome the difficult bit, all that these winning operations have left to do is maintain, maintain, maintain. Keep the standard going. Clock in, clock out, start again. Stay in the groove. Don't slip up. Focus.

And that, I'm afraid, is where too many of us tumble. We become lazy. A little bit of success spoils us. We lose focus. We stop trying as hard as we used to. We get tired of the task. Slowly but surely, the product degrades. And then, just as surely, it's gone. All that hard work of conception and launch, lost in the unwillingness to execute consistently.

There are no prizes for momentary excellence. You are either damn good most of the time or you're not. Offering an outstanding meal one time is meaningless if it descends to mediocre the next time the customer visits. Offering warm smiles and great hospitality is pointless if it's just for a week or when the right people are on duty. You do it all the time, or not at all. You're either all in together, or no one is. That's what excellence is. And that's why it's rare. It's difficult.

Businessfolk are usually quick to blame external factors when things go wrong. They will tell you economic downturns or unforeseen changes or unfair competition were their undoing. Not so. In my lifelong observation, the problems begin right inside. There are manifold internal failures: of leadership; of standard-setting; of employee engagement and staff retention; of working-capital management; of rigorous routines; of creating a workplace to be proud of. Statistical evidence bears this out. The death of a business is most often a case of suicide, not homicide.

Jules Goddard and Tony Eccles wrote an exceptionally insightful and delightfully irreverent book a few years ago: *Uncommon Sense, Common Nonsense*. In it, they pointed out that an astonishing 83 percent of company crises are caused by things that are internal and controllable. So much for the threat out there. The real enemy is within.

This rings true. My own experience of companies good and bad suggests we should be far more concerned about the dangers that are inside and all around us: failures of vision; refusals to see disruptive change

"

There are no prizes for momentary excellence. **You are either damn good most of the time or you're not.**

"

" The death of a business
is most often a case of
suicide, not homicide.
"

coming; bad boards; squabbling top teams; poor processes; low standards. Goddard and Eccles call these
"internal pathogens." They are swirling around in your
organization's bloodstream, too.

What Pays Off for the World Pays Off for You

Success for you is generally a direct function of value
for others. Create something that gives something.
Sell something worth buying. Shout a message worth
following. Give unrivalled utility to your customers;
incomparable careers to your employees; inimitable
responsibility to your employer; secure returns to your
investors. What pays off for the world pays off for you.
You don't generate prosperity in a vacuum; you do it in
an ecosystem. So extract yourself from yourself, and
dedicate yourself to giving value out. Then watch it
come back to you, multiplied.

Be Better First, Then **Be a Brand**

The most exhausting thing in life, I have discovered, is being insincere.

ANNE MORROW LINDBERGH

WHERE WE FIND THAT THE **SEARCH FOR MEANING** IS MORE IMPORTANT THAN THE SEARCH FOR BRANDING.

YOU ARE ASKED to believe some remarkable things these days: that a foodstuff can "give your children the confidence to face the future"; that a toothpaste will make very attractive members of the opposite sex flock around you in helpless abandon; that once you buy a certain type of life insurance you are protected from all the calamities that life can throw at you.

This is the purest type of hogwash. So why is it fed to us in the form of advertising, and why do we pay any attention to it? And worse, why do we allow such drivel to actually manipulate us into buying these products?

Advertising is meant to have a serious economic purpose. It is meant to provide information about products to the consumer, who can then make informed buying decisions. It is meant to allow producers to invest in their brand equity, which in turn protects consumers, because it means that any drop in product quality has disastrous financial consequences for the producer. In other words, the theory is that advertising actually empowers the consumer to buy better.

Oh yes? Theory and reality seem to have parted company some time ago. Better people than me have let loose on the practices of advertising, many years ago. The author H. G. Wells is rumoured to have called it "legalized lying." George Orwell went even further: advertising, said he, "is the rattling of a stick inside a swill-bucket."

Strong as these sentiments may be, it is difficult to disagree when we see what advertisers are up to these days. The principal preoccupation of advertising is to elevate mundane products from their banal surroundings and into rarefied realms. It's trying to turn shoes, toothpaste, deodorants and mobile phones into objects of nobility. It's sliding merchandise slyly into the arenas of philosophy and spirituality. That is why you will see adverts with children who gaze serenely into a future filled with joy, simply because their parents opened a certain bank account for them. Or a man whose soul is apparently stirred by the wonderfulness of his financial advisors. Or a fizzy drink whose consumption seems to have the power to unite the world and free it from strife.

You can give ordinary objects of consumption all the spin and polish you like. They remain mere objects. If we are going to improve our lives and our values, we will need to do more than just buy more stuff. There is more to the search for meaning than letting adverts lead you by the nose straight into the shopping mall. Yes, advertising and shopping are mainstays of the modern economy, but nobody ever said they have to be devoid of value and sincerity.

Buy Junk to Become a Hunk

The modern world is a non-stop kaleidoscope of manipulation. From the pages of magazines, the screens of televisions and the faces of the hideous billboards that disfigure the streets, the message is shouted out at us. Buy this mobile phone to find love in your life. Buy this soft drink to confirm the love you have for your children. Buy this detergent so that your family becomes cool and confident. Buy this, become that. Buy junk to become a hunk. Buy litter to become a hitter.

This kind of emotional manipulation debases the enterprise culture. It promotes intellectual laziness. It floats us away from solid ground and into a meaningless ether. We can now say anything about any product and be believed. We can bestow nobility on the trashiest of goods, merely by saying so—as long as we do it with style and panache. We no longer have to work as hard at making our products better and our processes efficient; merely hiring the right witchdoctor is often enough. Having the best advertising campaign (however divorced from reality) is the true competitive advantage. And quite often the consumer is left holding on to mere froth. That is why the landings are so hard and the disappointments so bitter.

If we accept this state of affairs, we are the dupes. Our despiritualized society is seeking consequence in bottles of perfume. Our buying classes are being led like rats by the seductive tunes of the new pied pipers. The mall is their place of worship, the product logo their deity. Where will it take us? There is no meaning to be had in conspicuous consumption. Meaning comes from honest toil, from an understanding of the value of kindness and compassion. Meaning comes from creating things of lasting value. Meaning comes from making investments in future generations, with little thought of present and personal reward.

No one wants to point this out, because everyone has a vested interest in the system. We all have jobs to protect, clients to service and targets to meet. The system lines our pockets, so we will do nothing to question it. We all have a small deal going on. But at some point in every person's life, the dream ends. The smoke clears, the mirrors crack, the curtain comes down. Then, we all have to start sifting through the debris of reality, seeking meaning in our soon-to-be-ended lives. What will we have to hold on to then?

Aldous Huxley, the great British thinker, recommended this: "Our business is to wake up... One must find a way of being in this world while not being of it." Making a point of sifting truth from lies would be a great start. We have made lying and evading a leadership habit. Is anyone telling you the truth? Our elected representatives seem to be liars for hire, willing to utter any blatant untruth that gives them allowances and rewards. Our appointed leaders seem to have no problem bending the truth beyond breaking point, telling us emphatically that that the hyena we have all been looking at is in fact a delightful butterfly, and repeating this ad nauseam. This is the era of fake news, fake elections, fake leaders, fake policies and fake outcomes. You can't believe a word you are told. Everything is suspect.

The business world is not immune from this disease. Once upon a time, the product sold itself. It had inherent attributes—functionality, quality, usefulness— which were all that a consumer needed to know about. It's all different now. Product is passé; the package prevails. So it's not enough to have a good product or good service. The consumer's perception of it is what must be managed. The brand is the thing. Investments must be made in mesmerizing adverts, seductive image associations and all sorts of manipulative stimulation of the consumer's latent sense cravings and insecurities.

What's the danger here? Again, that the emphasis is on the wrong things. Marketing, public relations and

> We have made lying and evading a leadership habit. **Is anyone telling you the truth?**

reputation management become the key functions—
not research, production or quality control. If those
boring "back-office" things are at all interesting, it is
for their impact on image and reputation. Otherwise,
they are just basic enabling functions. The sex, so to
speak, is in how to play with the consumer's mind.

Think about it. Have any of the following things
really changed in fundamental quality over the years:
soft drinks; alcoholic beverages; insurance; apparel?
Yet, if you believe their marketers, these products now
hold the key to enlightenment, moral uplift, personal
fulfilment and lifelong security for all the people who
care to buy them. It is the only way to make you buy
more, buy beyond saturation: by making you associ-
ate the product with a deeper value (community spirit,
say) or with a basic craving (usually sex or status), or by
making you fearful (of failure, or even death). This is
base manipulation. But you fall for it every time and buy
the product, thereby making the practice worthwhile.

Because vapid marketing works, shareholders support it and management teams revel in it. But often the
necessary investments in research, technology, quality, good people and strategic thought are sidelined or
forgotten. Some day, this neglect bites back, and bites
back hard.

In whichever country you live, I am sure you have
a leading bank with a seductive advertising campaign.
We all do. It probably shows a child facing a glowing

future. Yet I can wager that the promise of the campaign is not reflected in the banking halls, in product innovation, in strategic positioning or in basic decent customer service. I am willing to go further and state that the bank that invests the most in this kind of vapid advertising, unanchored from reality, is the one that will face the most issues in the boardroom and on the balance sheet in the years to come.

As individuals and as institutions, this kind of hollowness is a fate to avoid. Success does not come from elaborate smokescreens and special effects. At the end of the day, we have to develop some rather more dull and prosaic skill sets. We have to work hard, be consistent and keep raising our game. By simply playing with the packaging, we will ultimately be left with no product in our hands.

The Best Reputation to Have

Business leaders these days are bombarded with fresh advice regarding what might be their biggest asset: their reputation. They are asked to actively manage their reputations via heavy investments in public-relations contracts, brand building, social media engagement and "mind-share."

I have always found such advice to be wrong-headed and self-serving. There can be no doubt reputation is an extremely valuable thing. As companies and markets mature, importance moves away from tangibles (buildings, equipment, locations) to intangibles (reputation, customer loyalty, employee spirit). After a while, anyone can do the "tangibles thing," but few can pull off becoming distinctive through things that you can't even see or touch.

Reputation is one key intangible. No one denies its importance. Ask the corporate giants who have suffered huge reputation damage in recent years. If you don't protect your reputation, you can suffer near-death experiences. The best way to manage or improve your reputation, however, is where the problem lies.

The essential wisdom, surprisingly missing in our boardrooms, is this: you don't manage reputation by managing it directly; you manage it by working on the essentials of your business, which in turn influence your reputation. If you want to boost your reputation, in other words, boost your business basics—your efficiency, service levels, product quality, reliability and consistency.

Few managers want to hear this, since getting the basics right is hard work that takes years to accomplish. It's far more seductive to think you can gain a quick and relatively cheap reputation boost by having a savvy PR advisor, advertising guru or spin doctor. You can't. No amount of spin can turn a sow's ear into a silk purse.

This is a growing trend, and an unfortunate one—a flow of positive messages in traditional and social

media, about essentially bad companies. The thing
is this: people who run good businesses spend their
time running good businesses, not talking about them.
When products and services are great, that fact is
obvious. Reputation takes care of itself. Smart brand
management is then an additional layer of excellence,
not a shallow substitute for the real thing.

When the basics are bad, however—when quality
is shoddy, service is sour, reliability is non-existent—
no amount of massaging can get rid of that problem.
You have to fix the basics first. Feel-good advertising,
sugary social-media management, corporate social
responsibility projects or manipulation of online met-
rics will not help you. If your investors, employees and
customers don't have faith in you, your goose is cooked.
No amount of smoke or mirrors can get you out of that
one. The best reputation is not a wig or a smart suit; it
is a reflection of inner goodness.

Back to the One Thing

This takes us back to the "one thing" discussed in
Chapter 5—the thing that you absolutely must deliver
to your market. A power company, for example, has
only one brand promise: to provide reliable, affordable power to as many consumers as possible. That's it.
Connecting as many people as possible to the electrical

> The best reputation is
> not a wig or a smart suit;
> **it is a reflection of
> inner goodness.**

grid is the thing. If that promise is patently not being kept, a new logo; a new values statement; a swish, patriotic television advert; beautiful offices—all these mean nothing. If a power company that cannot supply power properly tries to emphasize these other things instead, it will evoke only anger and mockery as people question why the money is not used to just provide power. A brand is not what you portray, it's what you deliver.

All businesses should take note. Brand, firstly, is the business's one thing: its fundamental mandate. If that mandate is not delivered, the brand sucks, period. If the one thing is delivered, then brand moves on to being everything else—every manifestation of the organization that is felt by people in its ecosystem. For a bad power company, unanswered customer telephone lines are its brand. Sudden power cuts in the middle of important work or a favourite TV show are its brand. Long, snaking lines of customers trying to make payments are its brand.

For the rest of you, the same applies. That surly, indifferent receptionist is your brand. That vehicle driven badly with your logo on proud display is your brand. That convoluted refunds process is your brand. That unfriendly, out-of-date website is your brand. That tatty, crumpled billboard is your brand. That torn sofa in your reception is your brand. No logo, no advert, no social-media campaign can help those of you who ignore any of those things.

If your one thing stays strong—distinctively strong—you have a very good chance of making it through decades of turbulence.

When I was a boy, my mother always kept her sewing materials in a particular tin. That colourful round container was from Quality Street, the producers of a famous chocolate and toffee assortment. I'm pretty sure many of you are nodding your heads at that memory. Our mothers adored those handy boxes, as we adored the sweets.

Fast forward to today: my son loves the chocolates just like his father did (and does); our family always keeps the containers, once emptied of sweets, to store various household paraphernalia. Forty years later.

Those sweets look and taste pretty much exactly the same as they did all those years ago, and they still sell in huge numbers. Quality Street is the world's number-one-selling boxed chocolate assortment and is sold all over the globe. Their story began in 1890, when John Mackintosh opened a sweets shop in Halifax, in northern England. John's innovation was to combine hard toffee with soft caramel to produce the distinctive soft centres. His son Harold inherited the business, and in 1936 he invented Quality Street, which is still manufactured in the same facility today. Harold's revolution was to bring exotic chocolates to the people for a reasonable price, using a new twist-wrapping machine to wrap each piece of candy separately. He also used a tin to

A brand is not what you portray, **it's what you deliver.**

protect the aroma and freshness of the chocolates, and cannily saw that it would be reused in the household if made attractive and robust. Eighty years later, they're still going strong and still loved by new generations.

What's the one thing for a candy company? The taste of the products. Quality Street has kept to the same essential taste in its sweets, and it has paid off. For that, it has had to protect strict adherence to high quality standards for decades. I watch so many new players cut corners on quality within months of starting, let alone decades, and I wonder what they think they're doing.

You will not see many adverts for Quality Street. Yet there they are, probably in your local shop in many far-flung corners of the world. The product is the brand.

All for the Cameras

People making a large donation, smiling at the camera. People pretending to read their company's annual report together, for the camera. People wearing ill-fitting helmets while touring a construction site, pointing upwards for the camera. People sitting in a donated vehicle and pointing at the dashboard, for the camera. These are the very unimaginative public relations exercises many businesses undertake to show the world their wonderful activities.

Closely linked to PR is its cousin, CSR—corporate social responsibility. This is where companies make donations, help with needy causes, plant trees, et cetera, to convince the world they are good people with their hearts in the right place. All with the cameras flashing, of course.

I have two problems with all of this. First, those business pictures have looked exactly the same since I was a little boy. It's always donations being presented or pretend activities being set up for the cameras. For the love of imagination, can chief executives or PR agencies or photographers not come up with something new? Anything a little fresh, a little different, a little edgy? Because if businesses present themselves to the world in exactly the same tedious, banal and just plain boring way for decades, then what might be going on inside the business? The suspicion grows that their products, their management styles and their employment brands are also exactly the same. Stuck in time. Fossilized.

My second concern is more worrying. Is this all businesses can come up with when they want to communicate the good things they do? What is it with all the fakery—the feel-good donations, the self-conscious posturing, the maintaining of a sparkling public facade? Surely there's more going on than that?

The truth is, for way too many companies, the fakery is necessary because they are actually not good businesses. Too many are run purely as personal enrichment vehicles for their owners. Too many regard employees as expendable resources to be exploited and replaced as needed. Too many think customers are just suckers carrying wallets that must be emptied as quickly as possible. For those kinds of businesses, public displays of generosity or charity become necessary to paper over the cracks. A donation here, a staff visit there, all accompanied by some noble-sounding words, should do the trick.

As this book is trying to point out, business should be a far bigger deal than that. Corporations can make a great difference to the world. They can make life better for billions through their products. They can provide a lifetime of meaning and purpose to their employees. They can provide customers with everyday experiences filled with warmth and friendliness. Most choose not to, however. Most choose to be crafty, shrewd and small-hearted. And for them, the flashing cameras are a necessary confidence trick, some smoke and mirrors to hide the ugliness within.

In the private sector, truth is a scarce luxury. Most managers seem to live out an elaborate charade, one in which they pretend their companies exist to transform life on earth, where customers are always delighted and employees are always the most appreciated of assets. Rinse and repeat.

All over the public arena, lies are uttered with aplomb. It matters not whether you were caught on video or eye-witnesses are arrayed against you: you will splutter, laugh and bluster your way past all your accusers. And these days you will engage in relentless tweeting and endless PR and spin, rather than a sober examination and acceptance of the facts.

It need not be this way. If organizations wish to last for centuries, and if their promoters wish to do something bigger than just accumulate profits, then they must move away from the cameras and move toward doing things that truly matter, that have meaning. For that, the first step is to view this world as an arena in which to make a difference, not as a set of resources that must be exploited ruthlessly for personal gain. For most people, sadly, business is just about money, status and power—and it shows. Yet a company's chairperson or chief executive should be no different from a great artist or scientist, the leader of a movement, an upholder of values and standards. Then, products speak for themselves, employees become ambassadors and customers become evangelists. All of which is worth way more than a few PR pictures.

Where Do You Hang Your Values?

Walk into pretty much any organization's offices these days, and you'll see a statement of values hanging on the wall. Try it and see. I can predict pretty much what it says:

1. Excellence
2. Teamwork
3. Customer Focus
4. Corporate Citizenship
5. Integrity
6. Innovation

Is that your statement of values? Well, it's pretty much everyone's. Can you even remember what yours is? So what does it tell us about your organization? Pretty much nothing, since most organizations seem to have the exact same values. Which they can't remember, no matter how long the statement's been hanging on the wall.

Here's another question we never ask. Why do organizations hang these things on the wall? Most of us have values as people, or as families. Values we truly believe in. But has it ever occurred to you to hang a placard of values from your neck as you walk around? Or to put one on the family living room wall for visitors to see? I hope not...

The truth is, we don't have to display values we actually, truly believe in and live up to. People can see the values for themselves—in our everyday behaviour. If you are a person of integrity, you will prove it by being honest and ethical in all your dealings, not by creating a slogan about it. Similarly, if your family believes in hospitality, your visitors will see it in your warm

" Values are only interesting when they have entered hearts and minds. **When they can be felt, not read and forgotten.** "

welcomes and generous offerings, not in anything written on your wall.

Most organizations hang these things up everywhere because they don't really believe in them. They just need to pretend that they do. Let your company be different. If you truly centre your work on your customers, let your customers feel it, every day. If you want true excellence in your products, let your products speak for themselves. Too many of us are spinning the easy story of values rather than living up to the hard reality of embedding them. Values mean something when they are truly in the bloodstream of the entity, not hanging on its walls.

So where do you hang your values? On walls and on screensavers is the easy part. Values are only interesting when they have entered hearts and minds. When they can be felt, not read and forgotten.

Look beyond the hype, and you may discover that some of the very companies that show you the sugary stuff are the same ones that engage in a litany of bad practices: manipulating markets; breaching safety guidelines; suppressing employee dissent; fouling up the environment. Look away from the words that companies throw at you; look only at their actions. Companies should not just have values because they are a nice thing to show the world, or because a regulator is watching. Companies should have values because they are integral to good business, essential to longevity and central to strategy.

When it comes to values, stick to the ones you actually believe in, not the ones you think the world wants you to believe in. When you have identified your genuine values, protect them at all times, as jealously as you would the reputation of your child. Do not let them be besmirched by the seduction of short-term gain. Decades later, the value of embedding values in your very identity will become apparent.

Brand *You*

It's all the rage these days: how are you managing your brand?

Not your company or product brand, please understand: your personal brand. You, as a person and individual, now have to worry about how your brand is looking to the world. You will even be told to manage multiple sub-brands: your leadership brand, your employee brand, your family brand...

The idea is simple enough. Be aware that the world runs on perceptions and that you can manage perceptions. So don't just let your brand be what it will, blown this way and that; shape it and manage it. This is especially important in the era of mass connectivity and social media. We are now supposed to be very conscious of the digital streams that define us.

I have been asked about my own "brand" many times of late, and my response is always the same: I'm a person, not a brand. Let me focus on being a better person, and the brand will take care of itself. This can be a lonely view in a world dominated by marketing gurus and image managers, so it's always a pleasure to come across similar thoughts. Nilofer Merchant, an author, lecturer and director, wrote on the *Harvard Business Review* blog a few years back, "The truth is this: The brand follows the work. Your brand is the exhaust created by the engine of your life. It is a by-product of what happens as you share what you are creating, and with whom you are creating."

Wonderful words. Don't mistake the exhaust fumes for the engine. Don't spend all your time making the exhaust gases smell nice, be in the right colours or have pretty patterns. Look after the engine, and the emissions will be just fine. What we should all be preoccupied with is a search for meaning, not a search for branding. By focusing on image and perception, we are in severe danger of forgetting about substance.

Part of the issue comes from a widespread misconception about what a brand actually is. Those who get it know this: brand is not the spray job on the car or the ribbon on the package; brand is simply a manifestation of all the internal things we do, good and bad. Those who do many bad things have a lot of image management to do. Those who focus wholeheartedly on doing good don't have to worry much about managing perceptions: the good will shine through, most of the time. If you're going to worry more and more

"

What we should all be preoccupied with is a search for **meaning, not a search for branding.**

"

about your "packaging"—your appearance, where you are seen, what words you use and what associations you make—you are going to move away from what matters: the person within, the work that person does and the values that underpin the work.

What's true for corporations is true for persons: too much attention to brand, image and PR leads only to fakery and inauthenticity. We dress to impress, we craft every word for impact and we make sure we're seen in the right places. In my experience of the business world, those with too much budget for the packaging are precisely those with no budget for doing things right in the first place. People who are true to themselves are the only ones with any chance of doing things that matter. For the rest, the camera lights will eventually go out.

Be yourself, not a movie of yourself. Be the best person you can possibly be. Be flawed, because everyone is. Don't airbrush your flaws out; know them and minimize their negative impact. Be consistent and true to a core belief system. Be natural, not a fashion mannequin. Be true to your origins, not a ventriloquist's dummy that spews out insincere words in manufactured accents. Be all those things, and your brand will be just fine.

Let's end this chapter with a very unusual celebrity. Damien Rice is a strange kind of pop star. He achieved remarkable success years ago with his album

O, which went triple platinum in the UK and sold over two million copies in the rest of world. Yet, as he revealed in an interview at the time, his motivations were almost devoutly uncommercial. In Rice's own words, "It dawned on me recently that I'm going to die one day. And I started to wonder what, precisely, have I achieved in my life? A lot of people may know my name and my music, but so what? I'm still not the most compassionate or enlightened of people, and I want very much to become a better person. At some point, death is going to happen, and I must fill that void before it does."

The Bigger Deal, **Smaller**

"

There are no menial jobs, only menial attitudes.

WILLIAM J. BENNETT

WHERE WE MEET A
WHOLE BUNCH OF
BIG DEALERS.

I S THE BIGGER deal all about formidable, highly unusual people doing very bold, game-changing things? To think that is to miss the fact that all great movements in history stem from small actions from small people. Nothing starts off as a big deal until enough people start doing it.

This chapter takes *The Bigger Deal* from macro to micro, from large canvas to miniature. There are ordinary heroes and heroines in this world, people who do what is right repeatedly and successfully. Their voices and their example are lost to us because they do not court publicity and do not have public relations specialists deployed on their behalf.

Let's pick up the cudgels on behalf of the ordinary, decent, law-abiding, hard-working people of this planet. They are drowned out by loud and raucous people with media trains behind them. Let me tell you the stories of individual heroes and heroines I have met or learned of.

Happiness at 40 Degrees Celsius

Dubai in summer is no joke, and when my family and I arrived at the airport and stepped out of the air-conditioned car, it was like stepping into a furnace. Nonetheless, a porter came running up in the blinding heat to take our bags and load them onto his trolley. He did it quickly and cheerfully, even though he was awash with perspiration. He saw me looking at him with concern and stopped to make a wisecrack: "Sorry I'm so wet, sir—I just stepped out of the swimming pool!"

We entered the cool refuge of the terminal building with relief. Our ever-smiling porter waved enthusiastically at many people as we walked toward the check-in counter. He seemed to know pretty much every employee around him. They all waved back. He even chatted with passengers who were strangers to him, joking about how cold Dubai gets, but only indoors...

When we arrived at the check-in counter, my new friend placed all the suitcases onto the carousel, then went around to greet every single airline employee manning the various counters. He knew all their names, and they all chatted animatedly with him. He insisted on waiting until we were sorted out and ready to go toward the immigration area. Even then, he walked alongside, joking away. The tip was optional (he's an airline employee and the porter service is included in the fare), but I gave him the biggest tip I've ever given a porter. I suspect that happens to him a lot.

I asked him as we parted, "Why are you so happy?" His answer: "I am a happy person, sir. Why be unhappy? It's useless to be unhappy."

After I waved goodbye, I thought about this gentleman a lot over the next few hours. He is a Filipino, one of his country's many emigrants in Dubai and all over the world. Economic difficulty no doubt made him leave his homeland. His work is physical—loading, carrying, unloading—and he does this in a very oppressive climate. Every day he has to walk out of the oven that is the outdoors into the refrigerator that is the inside, and back, dozens of times.

Still that man keeps smiling. All the time. Still he makes time to appreciate everyone around him and lighten their daily load a little with a smile and a compliment. I trust his employers appreciate him, for he is a gem: someone who effortlessly builds relationships and strengthens the brand, every single day. So taken was I by the experience that I realized later to my regret that I had forgotten to note down his name. Had I done so, I would have written immediately to the airline to commend him and recommend a promotion for him.

Why so? Because people like these are rare indeed. Unlike most of us, they radiate instead of absorbing. They not only accept their lives as they are, but they embrace them—they make the most of every situation. My friend's fellow porters were all sullen and method-ical—efficient enough, but unable to feel good about such a trying job.

The Happiest Person in Your Organization

When I'm running seminars with corporate clients about the meaning of work, I sometimes ask this question: "Who is the most positive person in your organization?" Many hands often go up quickly. And most of the time, the same person is named. It's never the CEO. It's most often not even someone in senior management. The most positive person is often some-one way down there.

In one large automobile firm, dozens of hands came up very quickly in response to my question, and I heard the same name over and over. I was told of a man who worked as a clerical officer. His job was to take official vehicle papers to the government registration agency every morning and to come back to the office to file them properly every afternoon.

Can this really be the most motivated person in the organization?

The gentleman in question, I was told, greets every single colleague he meets by name and with a big smile, every morning. When he sets off on his daily walk to the government office every morning, he knows all the security guards and street vendors en route and chats with them about their children and the ebbs and flows of their daily lives. He is known by all the government officers he meets at his destination. Those fellows might be officious and forbidding with everyone else, but they always smile at our friend and never delay him unduly. When he's back in the office, our clerk has a daily ritual: he checks with HR to see if it's anyone's birthday that day, and then walks over to that person with a greeting and a small gift.

Intrigued by these stories, I made time to visit that auto company and meet the man himself. I sat down with a beaming, courteous chap, full of beans. I asked him why he felt so happy all the time. He assured me that his life was as full of difficulty and setbacks as anyone else's. But his next words resonated with those I had heard from the Dubai porter. Being cheerful is a choice. It is not that his life makes him cheerful; it is that he chooses to be cheerful in his life. Like the airport porter, my auto clerk does not see the point of being miserable. Life is unlivable if you let it depress you, he told me. It's better to be smiling. And to make others smile.

And that's a bigger deal, right there.

In our families, our communities and our institutions, the happy people are pure gold. They are not always exuberant extroverts, please note: my friend certainly was, but many happy people radiate a quieter

"

In our families, our communities and our institutions, the happy people are pure gold. **Our collective human spirit is richer because of them.** „

kindness that is just as effective. The point is, their energy is directed outward. Look around you. These good people exist, and they make life better for everyone. Our collective human spirit is richer because of them.

Too many folks are the opposite of this. They expect others to make life right for them; they whine and groan about their condition, no matter how privileged; they spread ill-will and negativity; they absorb kindness without gratitude and radiate toxicity in return.

I know many well-to-do people who have it all but still manage to look stressed-out and feel victimized every day. They always have someone to blame for their perceived plights and slights; they bring everyone around them down. They kill all signs of enthusiasm in their ambit. These characters are the opposite of my porter and clerk friends. They should be avoided and kept away from positions of authority.

So how are you feeling today, and will you be adding to the happiness in the world or depleting it?

The Kiosk of Kindness

Many moons ago, a gentleman called Chege ran a food kiosk close to the main campus of the University of Nairobi. Chege's place was well frequented by students and was an institution unto itself. Many of these students came from relatively humble backgrounds from all over Kenya and lacked support systems in the big, unfriendly city. The meagre "boom" (living) allowance they were given soon ran out, and toward the month-end many students did not have sufficient funds to have three meals per day.

Chege was a godsend at those times of the month, for he could offer a big mug of steaming tea and two very thick slices of bread with margarine—a meal that could sustain many a stomach for the rest of the day. But Chege had another attribute: he was very kind-hearted by nature. Unlike his fellow businessmen, Chege had a soft spot for these struggling students. Many of them could turn to Chege at the most difficult times and ask for some food on credit. Chege would often oblige. He ran credit accounts with many a student, and they loved him for it.

A question: Was it wise for Chege to offer credit to the student community? It was certainly not shrewd—few businessmen I know would take a risk with such an un-creditworthy group. "Pay cash or take a hike" would be the normal policy. Sound business practice is about profit maximization, is it not? Those students would take advantage and never repay poor old Chege, don't you think?

That's not how it worked out, though. Chege's beneficiaries mostly repaid him. Years later, Chege aged and wished to leave the ugly, noisy, corrupt city and retire to his rural home. But he had no means of generating income back in his rustic abode, and so he remained stuck in the city.

A benefactor appeared. One of the students who had benefited from Chege's kind heart years back had never forgotten it. He was now a well-regarded professional with a thriving practice. When he heard of Chege's quandary, he showed up at the kiosk and offered Chege enough money to pack up in Nairobi and start a whole new venture back home. A surprised and very grateful Chege accepted.

This heartwarming tale was told to me by a student of that era, himself a beneficiary of Chege's informal credit facilities. I was told there are many like him, part of the city's movers and shakers today.

What's the lesson here? Do people favours, so that someday one of them might do you a big one back? Not at all. Chege had no way of knowing that's how things would work out for him. The real lesson is about unsolicited kindness. Most of us become hardened against being kind, particularly when we live in a "me and mine" society. Those of us who run businesses become even more flinty, suspecting every customer of being a fraudster and thinking it dumb to do favours in business. The only good turns we do offer are of the "you do something for me and I'll do something for you" variety.

A great life is not like that, nor is a great business. Keeping a part of your heart open for strangers is an essential part of being human. Helping people randomly, with no hope of a "return" on this "investment," is an extremely wise thing to do. Good is not brought into the world by wishing others would do it; it is by doing it yourself, in the smallest but most sincere way. You may never become materially rich like this, but you will certainly become very wealthy. Your wealth will be the pool of decency and kindness in the world, and the success of the people you helped when they needed it most. And when the final tally is done of whose life was more meaningful, you will be way ahead of most folks around you.

The Sweeper Who Wasn't Swept Away

Let's continue to showcase common people who show uncommon wisdom, unknown people who need to be known, and little people who are actually very, very big.

Allow me to introduce a special lady to you. She is called Yu Youzhen, and she lives in the city of Wuhan in China. I wrote about her in my weekly newspaper column some years back when she came to world attention. Yu has done hard physical labour for four decades. She has, at various times, been a farmer, cook, truck driver and street sweeper. Her job involves working long hours, six days a week, sweeping the streets of her city. When I wrote about her, she was earning the

"

Good is not brought into
the world by wishing
others would do it; it
is by doing it yourself,
**in the smallest but
most sincere way.**

"

equivalent of USD 200 per month. Her son worked as a driver and her daughter sat at a cinema kiosk, both earning similar amounts.

Something else you need to know about Yu: she is a millionaire. Some time back, Yu received a sudden windfall. Her family land in Donghu village was bought by the government for a property development. Yu wisely invested the money in property in the city, and she now owns seventeen apartments worth more than a million US dollars.

Why would this lady, seemingly of sound mind, want to carry on working as a sweeper? She was interviewed by a local Chinese newspaper, and she said the following: "Work is not just about the salary, it makes one focused. Laziness gives rise to all sorts of bad habits." She continued, "I want to be a role model for my children... I do not want to sit around idly and eat up my fortune... My son once stayed at home for two months, and I kept scolding him during that time. Now he is doing pretty well. He said to me later I was right. I was worried he would hang out with bad people and ruin our family."

I trust you can see that we are listening to a rare wisdom. A million dollars in assets, plus lucrative rental flows? How many people you know would resist the temptation to stop working altogether and just sit back and "enjoy" life for a "change"? But Yu has a different motivation. First, she sees the intrinsic value of work.

She is a good worker, rated highly by her supervisors. She finds focus and purpose in work. She finds satisfaction in a job well done, to a high personal standard. Whether that job is sweeping or surgery, the mere fact of doing it properly really, really matters. Second, she's doing the job she knows. Rather than reinvent her life in her fifties, she would rather stay in the groove she has created for herself, instead of making risky experiments. Rental income provides her with a secure safety net. Lastly, she wants to set this example for her children. She understands the dangers of laziness and lack of purpose. She wants her children to find joy in labour, as she does.

Contrast this with what so many do with sudden windfalls: blow it on parties to impress friends; invest it in precarious business ventures with unreliable partners; go on a shopping splurge that provides a short-lived high and fritters away the asset.

What would you do in Yu's place? It's worth asking yourself that question, for the answer will bring your core values to the surface. What matters to you, truly? What are you aiming for? In what does meaning reside in your life? You don't have to follow Yu's path, but do recognize that it is a good and meaningful one. It places good work done well at the centre of human existence. I suspect Yu sleeps a lot more peacefully than most of us.

Love What You Do

Porters. Clerks. Hawkers. Sweepers. All the ordinary folk highlighted in this chapter are not ordinary at all. They have a very big deal going on, in very common-place ways. Through acceptance, through cheerfulness, through positivity, through dedication, through kind-ness. Their greatness is in the daily uplift they bring to all those in their orbit.

Are they doing what they love? "Do what you love" is the exhortation commonly heard these days. Every motivational speaker urges you to find your passion; every pushy tweet pushes you to discover your true aptitude—that is how you will do your best work. The late Steve Jobs, in his now legendary address at Stanford University, told us, "Don't settle." That sends many of us searching for our true vocation, the work that will ignite our latent passion.

It is true that many of life's truly outstanding achievements are clocked by people who feel fervent, unbridled zest for what they do. Without this magic nectar, we are merely competing for mediocrity. Listen to a truly great singer singing. Note the effect the song is having on you. Now listen to the same song rendered by a more ordinary artiste. Note the difference in what you feel. The first singer probably invoked deep emo-tions in you, heightened your senses and made you feel better, even euphoric, about the world. The second? Well, it's just a song.

It is easy to attribute the discrepancy to God-given talent. Certainly, there are differences in natural ability that become apparent at a young age. But there's something much more important happening here. There's a magic nectar at work. It's called passion. The truly great singer is always and in all ways in love with her craft. She has immersed herself fully in her song. How well she sings that song matters more than anything else in the world to her. She's committed, lock, stock and barrel. She has, in fact, become the song.

Watch accountants at work. Most are merely adding up columns and following arcane rules, and then collecting their reward at month-end. A precious few, however, are passion-play accountants. They absolutely love what they do. They would rather do it than anything else in the world. They adore the way the numbers behave when tickled. They understand deeply the business story that creates the numbers. You'll know when you meet such an accountant (but don't hold your breath waiting).

An ordinary cook assembles ingredients and mixes them in accordance with a recipe. A truly great chef throws his own heart into the pot every time, and feels genuine, wrenching pain when the result is inadequate. An ordinary writer lines up letters on a page. A truly passionate one makes them dance across, and into your head. Look around you. Whether you observe a shoeshine boy, a chief executive, a biologist, a poet or a photographer, it's the passion people who produce the

" Those who are wholeheartedly in love with their work need to do their thing, only their thing and no other thing, and do it to the highest possible level of achievement before they're done. **"**

real results. If you want limits tested, boundaries broken, borders breached, frontiers affronted—you have to look to the people who love their work with unyielding fire. You have to find the equivalent of the mother's laser-like focus on her child.

Is passion enough? No. You must also develop a deep capability, and that takes application. Too many talented folks don't feel strongly enough for the subject of their talent. They don't dive deep; they swim on the surface, looking around for other pools to dip into. Those who are wholeheartedly in love with their work, however, will never look around. They have blinders on. They need to do their thing, only their thing and no other thing, and do it to the highest possible level of achievement before they're done.

Does passion always yield success? Again, no. Sometimes, the world does not value the thing you're passionate about and won't reward you for it, at least in your lifetime. At other times, the passion creates a self-absorbed madness that yields no benefit to the world and consumes its bearer. But so what? The trying is the thing. For the passion people, it is better to explode and go down in flames than to choke slowly to death in the ashes of timidity.

If you don't understand that last sentence, don't fret. It wasn't written for you. It was written to make the mad-passion people dance, and I suspect a few are twirling.

You may have a question, though. If passion-inflamed purpose is the key to this kind of success, how do we find the thing that will ignite our passion? How do we know when we have found the occupation that will preoccupy us for the rest of our days and give us a shot at greatness? How will I know what I have been put on this planet to do? What if I never discover the thing I should have spent my life doing?

I have several answers for this conundrum. The most important point is that your true vocation is not something you design or choose; it chooses you. The people who have an abiding passion for something just have it. They feel it from a young age and spend their lives agitating to be allowed to spend more time doing that thing that most seduces them. It could be the joy of art, the thrill of numbers, the mystery of science— but it usually casts its spell early.

If you are in the group of people who don't feel the thrill, however, perhaps you need to dig a little deeper. What are the signs that you might be doing the thing that you will love? Here are some personal views.

The first is that you will stop noticing time. When you are immersed in the thing that matters most to you, you are not always looking at the clock to know when to move on to something else. Our life's most important work sucks us in every time we do it, and we emerge, a little bedraggled and confused, hours later, wondering when it got dark.

"

It is better to explode and go down in flames than to choke slowly to death in the ashes of timidity. "

The second sign is that it won't feel like work when you're doing it. You will not be that concerned about what you're getting paid, or how long you're taking, or how boring it all is. There is nothing else you'd rather be doing. For passion people, work-life balance is a strange concept. Work is life. If you wake up happy to start working, you will know what I mean.

The third sign is that you don't feel any incongruence, any misalignment, when you're working. Your work fits with your fundamental goals and values as a person. You feel at ease. Your life just fits. Finding your passion is finding yourself. Be very careful about this one. Often, what we think is our passion is just something we have absorbed from popular culture. We think it ought to be our passion because that is what the world respects.

Alain de Botton warned in a 2009 TED Talk, "A lot of the time our ideas about what it would mean to live successfully are not our own. They're sucked in from other people. And we also suck in messages from everything from the television to advertising to marketing, et cetera. These are hugely powerful forces that define what we want and how we view ourselves. What I want to argue for is not that we should give up on our ideas of success, but that we should make sure that they are our own."

If you've found work that lets time fly by unnoticed, that doesn't feel like work and that feels like it's you—congratulations. Passionate engagement, however, is not the norm. For most people, working life is a drudgery, a necessary evil. They work just to earn their daily bread. They work to earn money so that they can come to life elsewhere. Those consumed by passion have no choice but to do their thing. But the vast majority of mankind may never experience euphoria in their work. That's okay, too. Not everyone can be the blazing comet who's found the right vocation; you can also be passionate about the *way* you do things. Passion is not reserved purely for the artistic genius or the mad scientist. Whatever you're doing, for as long as you're doing it, do it to the best of your ability and with all your heart. Your life will be immeasurably richer, and many self-discoveries will be made.

Bill Shankly was a legendary soccer manager. For me his most important utterance is this: "If I was a road-sweeper, my street would be the cleanest in the borough." Passion is also about personal standards: how you do it, not just what you do. If life does not give us the luxury of doing what we love, we must learn to love what we do.

For some of us, the magical match between work and passion will happen naturally. For many more, meaning will come not from love of the work, but from an acceptance of the necessity of work, and of doing it well and with good spirit. And for most, work may remain just drudgery, a necessary stream

" If life does not give us the luxury of doing what we love, **we must learn to love what we do.** "

of income, something that enables us to come alive elsewhere. Then, the bigger deal emerges from our relationships, our hobbies and pastimes, our duties and responsibilities.

Find it where you will, but find your bigger deal.

Thank You

Let us end this chapter with some thanks. Let us thank those who are polite and courteous, even when everyone around them is rude and obnoxious. Those who maintain etiquette and decorum, even though that doesn't get you anywhere in this increasingly ugly world. Those who say "please" and "thank you," even though no one says it to them.

Let us be grateful for those who maintain road discipline and manners, even when every cretin around them is mounting pavements, gesturing obscenely, cutting in rudely and overtaking dangerously. Let us thank those who still give way, dip their lights, use their indicators and wait patiently for the traffic to clear.

Let us express our gratitude for those who still try to run their businesses honestly. Those who don't evade taxes, who try to create a genuinely good product or service, who compete legitimately by offering better value. They are a dying race, surrounded as they are by dodgers, scammers and corrupters masquerading as businesspeople.

Let us record our debt to those few remaining civil servants who still work with a sense of public duty, who do their jobs to a high standard and hold the fort against the networks of patronage all around them. They are in there, deep in the heart of the system. They are underpaid and undervalued. But they matter.

Let us recognize those honest, public-spirited bravehearts who go to the polls every few years to try to become representatives of the people, presidents even. These courageous crusaders haven't got a hope in hell of winning, since they actually campaign on issues and integrity rather than ethnic vitriol, cheap handouts and false promises. They will finish in fifth place at best, whilst rabble-rousers and snake-oil salesmen are re-elected. Because our unsung heroes do not give out tee shirts or arrive in large convoys or dole out flowery promises, they will never be voted in. But they keep trying. And thank goodness they do; otherwise, the only voices heard would be of loudmouths and hate-speakers.

And finally, let us sing a word of appreciation for those who just smile. It is hard to do that in this brutish, uncouth world, where customers are rude and arrogant and bosses are worse. It is hard to smile when scowlers get every promotion and win every prize. But there are many who smile in greeting and in farewell, and smile in between. Thank all that is good for their presence, for without them we would all live in a snapping, barking hell.

"

Good people don't
descend into the mire;
they rise above it.

"

We must thank all these people because they are the only ones holding on to the cloak of civilization, whilst the rest do their damnedest to descend back to jungle rule. Without decent, honest and considerate folk in our midst, we would be no better than grunting beasts killing one other for every scrap of self-gain.

Why do they do it, these decent folk, when there is nothing to gain from it? The answer is simple. They do it for themselves. They do it because they have dignity to protect, values they believe in, a standard they will not drop. Their behaviour does not depend on the behaviour around them. Just because everyone is a boor is no reason for these good-hearted folks to be the same. Good people don't descend into the mire; they rise above it. There is great peace to be had in personal dignity.

And so, please join me in thanking all the good people. They make the world still worth living in; they keep hope burning; they give everyone a reason to carry on. If they didn't exist, neither would anyone else, for the world would be in flames.

Perhaps you could even thank one of the good people in person, and do it today.

Conclusion
Make Yourself Matter

Success is liking yourself, liking what you do, and liking how you do it.

MAYA ANGELOU

WE ARE SURROUNDED by Bureaucrats, Note Takers, Literalists, Manual Readers, TGIF Labourers, Map Followers, and Fearful Employees." That's Seth Godin describing what most people in the world do in his very inspiring book, *Linchpin*.

So look at the list and answer: Isn't that what you do? Exercise brainless bureaucracy created by others? Take notes while others tell you the answers? Take everything literally as you see it on the page? Read manuals to work out what to do in your world? Follow maps, rather than strike out into uncharted territory? Sit in fear at your workplace, because you know you could be laid off on someone's whim?

It's a frightening list, and unfortunately it covers most of us. Even high-powered lawyers, marketers, doctors, accountants, engineers and architects are not spared. If you are generally following someone else's instructions, doing brainless cut-and-paste work, following the rules laid down by long-dead people and just living for your weekends and your holidays... then you are in some trouble.

I had the privilege of spending some time with Seth when he visited Nairobi some years back, and he pointed out something: that world is over. The old contract, where you did what you were told and the system looked after you by giving you job security, health care and a pension, is irredeemably broken. Ask the hundreds of thousands of bankers whom global banking giants regularly announce they are laying off (while declaring bumper profits). Those are all folks who followed orders—until they were ordered out of the door. For a while, the contract worked. If you obeyed, you were looked after. That's gone, and it's been blown away by technology, connectivity and ferocious competition. Now, if you (or your child) are planning to just play the game, you are in for some serious shocks.

So what are you going to do? The answer is to become a "linchpin"—someone who can't just be tossed casually out of something. Whether you have a job or run your own business, you must become indispensable. The people around you—employers, colleagues, customers—must value you greatly. You must bring something unusual, something original, something valuable to the party. You must matter. If you're just a face in the crowd, you might be dispersed along with that crowd anytime.

Now, this has always been true. It's just that it's become a whole lot truer in recent years. The challenge for us all is how to matter, and that requires a whole new mindset. Instead of looking to blend in, we need to stand out. Instead of being part of the conventional wisdom, we need to be part of the uncommon sagacity.

I hope that, in the course of reading this book, the nature of the bigger deal has become apparent. The bigger deal happens when an individual structures the deal to deliver results for other people, to work for a greater good, to do something that has lasting value. Politicians who grab hold of their people and take them on a journey of shared prosperity and common development are engaged in a bigger deal. Businessfolk who make an actual difference in the lives of their customers, who solve their problems or make them happier or more productive, are delivering a bigger deal. Employers who engage with employees as though they are on a shared mission that everyone can believe in are connecting to a bigger deal. Employees who give their work their all, not to make a great impression or to wangle a promotion, but simply because it matters to them personally to do things properly, are dealing big.

Ordinary people who do good not because it looks good, but because they *are* good, are living the bigger deal. Any person on earth who, by the example of their life, makes other people want to be better or bigger is playing big every day.

Six Ways to Play Bigger

To close this book, here is a six-point guide to what might make genuine riches come your way and to carving out a bigger deal for yourself.

First point: *Believe* that you can play bigger. Do you dare to matter? If not, stop reading now and carry on with your life as is.

Second point: *Come alive!* Most of us are not truly alive at all; we are merely sleepwalking through life. We are going through the motions, putting up appearances, parroting all the right stuff. But are we alive? No. We are in a dream. So before you do anything else, wake up and ignite yourself. Without zest, no true success can come for you. Get to the place where you'll be awake and fully engaged.

Third point: Give most things you do your *best shot.* Not your not-bad shot or your pretty-good shot; your best shot. Don't save your energy; expend it fully in what you're doing. Go for it, and don't hold back. Plunge in. Half-interested is fully wasted. If you think it's worth doing, it's worth doing at full tilt. Make a mistake, start over, but don't stand dithering on the starting line. If you are in a job, give it an extra shot of enthusiasm. Do your work better than anyone else.

Step back and rethink: Why is it done this way? What would make it better? Solve and resolve things, rather than just complain about them. What do you have to lose by coming alive? Either you'll become indispensable to your current organization or you'll get the hell out and do your unusual thing somewhere else, where you can be allowed to matter. Either way, you win.

Fourth point: *Don't be alone.* Results only come through others. You need people. Even if you're highly individualistic by nature or occupation, you will only matter through the collective. Connect and engage with the people around you. Infect them with your passion. Understand them as humans. Get them to do their best work, and your own best work will also emerge.

Fifth point: *Focus the beam.* It is very tempting to flash the torch everywhere and to start chasing after every interesting shadow out there. There's a time to look around and try many things out, but if you keep doing it all your life it is the single most effective way not to be successful. Find your spot. Find the place where you can combine great enthusiasm with genuine distinctive capability. Stay on that spot. Make your performance on that spot the best you can possibly make it. Don't keep flashing and flitting. You can be the best at something, but only mediocre at everything.

My last point: Create value for *others.* As Chapter 5 of this book elaborated, success for you is generally a direct function of value for others. Create something that gives something. Sell something worth buying.

"

Get them to do their best work, and your **own best work will also emerge.**

"

Give it out, over and over. Value to your customers, growth to your employees, dedication to your employers, reward to your investors. What pays off for the world pays off for you. Get out of yourself, and give something out. What you give will make its way back to you.

These six entreaties are not a nice bit of theory, a meaningless speaker's spiel, a vibrant-but-vapid message. I live by them, and they guided the writing of this very book you are reading. I watch them play out every day in the people and organizations I work with or study. So test them out for yourself. Give them a go, and you may find yourself answering the question I asked at the beginning of this book:

What's the point of your life? Do you know?

A word before you go: If your ambition is merely to make money, you may ignore this book entirely. If personal gain is all you want, you've just wasted precious hours reading it. Become a drug dealer, a pimp, a peddler of patronage, a parasite. Those ways are way quicker and will help you build the fat bank account you crave.

If, however, you are here to make an altogether bigger deal of your life; if you want meaning more than you want mammon; if you want to leave a mark on this planet—then please do try to create something that is bigger than yourself and that will outlast you. It may become your life's signature achievement.

Thank You

I T TOOK ME several years to write this book. I was plagued with questions of meaning: Does it need to be written? Does it help anyone? Is it just a set of exhortations that can't be put into practice? Is it frothy "self-help" that masquerades as advice?

And yet as I parked and restarted the book, I noticed something: it was getting written anyway—in my weekly column for Kenya's *Sunday Nation*, as a procession of tweets that would riff out of me from time to time and as a recurring theme in my talks and seminars. I realized that when you need to write something, you will write it anyway and any which way.

Those who follow my regular outpourings will, therefore, notice they are on familiar ground. The book unites the many threads I have been weaving over the past few years into, I hope, a single tapestry. It is more a bringing-together than an act of creation. Yet there is much also that is entirely new, provoked by the act of mingling and melding.

My gratitude, then, to my editors at the Nation Media Group who have allowed me free rein to express my own bigger deal on my Sunday page for many years. Some of what is now here was there first. My thanks also to the multitudes of Twitter followers who engaged with, argued with and added to the many tweets that were some of the seeds of this book. If used well, social media provides an author with the unprecedented opportunity to test every thought out in the market and to have it brought down to earth.

Lastly, a book is only a book when it leaves its author and becomes a real thing out in the world, ready to be opened. For that last part, I am very grateful to Page Two Books and their singularly enthusiastic and very capable team. That's a bigger deal right there.

Sunny Bindra works as a "sense-maker"—he helps leaders and organizations understand their worlds and succeed in them. He is a business advisor, speaker, writer and educator. He has designed and led business-school programs in strategy and board governance, and is the founder of Fast Forward, Eastern Africa's premier leadership programme. *The Bigger Deal* is his third book.

www.sunwords.com

f | ⟨O⟩ | ⟨Y⟩ | @sunnysunwords

9 789966 120434